Student Workbook to Accompany

Administrative Procedures *for Medical Assisting* Third Edition

Kathryn A. Booth RN-BSN, MS, RMA, RPT
Total Care Programming, Inc., Palm Coast, Florida

Leesa G. Whicker, BA, CMA (AAMA)
Central Piedmont Community College, Charlotte, North Carolina

Terri D. Wyman, CPC, CMRS
UMASS Memorial Medical Center, Worcester, Massachusetts

Donna Jeanne Pugh, RN, MSN/ED
University of Florida College of Nursing, Jacksonville, Florida

Sharion Thompson, BS, RMA
Bryant and Stratton College, Cleveland Area, Parma, Ohio

McGraw-Hill Higher Education

Boston Burr Ridge, IL Dubuque, IA New York San Francisco St. Louis
Bangkok Bogotá Caracas Kuala Lumpur Lisbon London Madrid Mexico City
Milan Montreal New Delhi Santiago Seoul Singapore Sydney Taipei Toronto

Student Workbook to accompany
ADMINISTRATIVE PROCEDURES FOR MEDICAL ASSISTING, THIRD EDITION
Kathy Booth, Leesa Whicker, Terri Wyman, Donna Jeanne Pugh, and Sharion Thompson

Published by McGraw-Hill, a business unit of The McGraw-Hill Companies, Inc., 1221 Avenue of the Americas, New York, NY 10020.

2 3 4 5 6 7 8 9 0 QPD/QPD 0 9 8

ISBN 978-0-07-321145-9
MHID 0-07-321145-1

Cover credit: Woman with glasses browsing paper files: ©Image Source Black Copier, Computer, screenshot, person talking on the phone and writing: Kathryn Booth. Background: David Gould, ©Gettyimages

www.mhhe.com

Contents

Preface

The *Student Workbook* provides you with an opportunity to review and master the concepts and skills introduced in your student textbook, *Medical Assisting: Administrative and Clinical Procedures Including Anatomy and Physiology,* Third Edition. Chapter by chapter, the workbook provides the following:

Vocabulary Review, which tests your knowledge of key terms introduced in the chapter. Formats for these exercises include Matching, True or False, and Passage Completion.

Content Review, which tests your knowledge of key concepts introduced in the chapter. Formats for these exercises include Multiple Choice, Sentence Completion, and Short Answer.

Critical Thinking, which tests your understanding of key concepts introduced in the chapter. These questions require you to use higher-level thinking skills, such as comprehension, analysis, synthesis, and evaluation.

Applications, which provide opportunities to apply the concepts and skills introduced in the chapter. For example, using role play, you will perform such activities as developing a personal career plan and interviewing a medical specialist.

Case Studies, which provide opportunities to apply the concepts introduced in the chapter to lifelike situations you will encounter as a medical assistant. For example, you may be asked to decide how to respond to a patient who calls the doctor's office to say that she is having difficulty breathing or you may be requested to give information about the thyroid gland to a patient who has just been referred for thyroid testing.

Procedure Competency Checklists, which enable you to monitor your mastery of the steps in the procedure(s) introduced in a chapter, such as Preparing a Patient Medical Record/Chart and Performing a Surgical Scrub. Answers to the material in the *Student Workbook* are found in the *Instructor's Resource Binder.* Ask your instructor to let you check your work against these answers.

Together, your student textbook and the *Student Workbook* form a complete learning package. *Medical Assisting: Administrative Procedures,* Third Edition will prepare you to enter the medical assisting field with the knowledge and skills necessary to become a useful resource to patients and a valued asset to employers and to the medical assisting profession.

Medical Assisting Reviewers

Roxane M. Abbott, MBA
Sarasota County Technical Institute
Sarasota, FL

Dr. Linda G. Alford, Ed.D.
Reid State Technical College
Evergreen, AL

Suzzanne S. Allen
Sanford Brown Institute
Garden City, NY

Ann L. Aron, Ed.D.
Aims Community College
Greeley, CO

Emil Asdurian, MD
Bramson ORT College
Forest Hills, NY

Rhonda Asher, MT, ASCP, CMA
Pitt Community College
Greenville, NC

Adelina H. Azfar, DPM
Total Technical Institute
Brooklyn, OH

Joseph H. Balatbat, MD, RMA, RPT, CPT
Sanford Brown Institute
New York, NY

Mary Barko, CMA, MAED
Ohio Institute of Health Careers
Elyria, OH

Katie Barton, LPN, BA
Savannah River College
Augusta, GA

Kelli C. Batten, NCMA, LMT
Medical Assisting Department Chair
Career Technical College
Monroe, LA

Nina Beaman, MS, RNC, CMA
Bryant and Stratton College
Richmond, VA

Kay E. Biggs, BS, CMA
Columbus State Community College
Columbus, OH

Norma Bird, M.Ed., BS, CMA
Medical Assisting Program Director/Master Instructor
Pocatello, ID

Kathleen Bode, RN, MS
Flint Hills Technical College
Emporia, KS

Natasha Bratton, BSN
Beta Tech
North Charleston, SC

Karen Brown, RN, BC, Ed.D
Kirtland Community College
Roscommon, MI

Kimberly D. Brown, BSHS, CHES, CMA
Swainsboro Technical College
Swainsboro, GA

Nancy A. Browne, MS, BS
Washington High School
Kansas City, KS

Teresa A. Bruno, BA
EduTek College
Stow, OH

Marion I. Bucci, BA
Delaware Technical and Community College
Wilmington, DE

Michelle Buchman, BSN, RNC
Springfield College
Springfield, MO

Michelle L. Carfagna, RMA, ST, BMO, RHE
Brevard Community College
Cocoa, FL

Carmen Carpenter, RN, MS, CMA
South University
West Palm Beach, FL

Pamela C. Chapman, RN, MSN
Caldwell Community College and Technical Institute
Hickory, NC

Patricia A. Chappell, MA, BS
Director, Clinical Laboratory Science
Camden County College
Blackwood, NJ

Phyllis Cox, MA Ed, BS, MT(ASCP)
Arkansas Tech University
Russellville, AR

Stephanie Cox, BS, LPN
York Technical Institute
Lancaster, PA

Christine Cusano, CMA, CPhT
Clark University-CCI
Framingham, MA

Glynna Day, M.Ed
Dean of Education
Academy of Professional Careers
Boise, ID

Anita Denson, BS
National College of Business and Technology
Danville, KY

Leon Deutsch, RMA, BA, MA Ed
Keiser College
Orlando, FL

Walter R. English, MA, MT(AAB)
Akron Institute
Cuyahoga Falls, OH

Dennis J. Ernst MT(ASCP)
Center for Phlebotomy Education
Ramsey, IN

C.S. Farabee, MBA, MSISE
High-Tech Institute Inc.
Phoenix, AZ

Deborah Fazio, CMAS, RMA
Sanford Brown Institute-Cleveland
Middleburg Heights, OH

William C. Fiala, BS, MA
University of Akron
Akron, OH

Cathy Flores, BHS
Central Piedmont Community College
Charlotte, NC

Brenda K. Frerichs, MS, MA, BS
Colorado Technical University
Sioux Falls, SD

Michael Gallucci, PT, MS
Assistant Professor of Practice,
Program in Physical Therapy,
School of Public Health,
New York Medical College
Valhalla, NY

Susan C. Gessner, RN, BSN, M Ed
Laurel Business Institute
Uniontown, PA

Bonnie J. Ginman, CMA
Branford Hall Career Institute
Springfield, MA

Robyn Gohsman, RMA, CMAS
Medical Career Institute
Newport News, VA

Cheri Goretti, MA, MT(ASCP), CMA
Quinebaug Valley Community College
Danielson, CT

Jodee Gratiot, CCA
Rocky Mountain Business Academy
Caldwell, ID

Marilyn Graham, LPN
Moore Norman Technology Center
Norman, OK

Donna E. Guisado, AA
North-West College
West Covina, CA

Debra K. Hadfield, BSN, MSN
Baker College of Jackson
Jackson, MI

Carrie A. Hammond, CMA, LPRT
Utah Career College
West Jordan, UT

Kris A. Hardy, CMA, RHE, CDF
Brevard Community College
Cocoa, FL

Toni R. Hartley, BS
Laurel Business Institute
Uniontown, PA

Brenda K. Hartson, MS, MA, BS
Colorado Technical University
Sioux Falls, SD

Marsha Perkins Hemby, BA, RN, CMA
Pitt Community College
Greenville, NC

Linda Henningsen, RN, MS, BSN
Brown Mackie College
Salina, KS

Carol Hinricher, MA
University of Montana College of Technology
Missoula, MT

Elizabeth A. Hoffman, MA Ed., CMA
Baker College of Clinton Township
Clinton Township, MI

Gwen C. Hornsey, BS
Medical Assistant Instructor
Tulsa Technology Center, Lemley Campus
Tulsa, OK

Helen J. Houser, MSHA, RN, RMA
Phoenix College
Phoenix, AZ

Melody S. Irvine, CCS-P, CPC, CMBS
Institute of Business and Medical Careers
Ft. Collins, CO

Kathie Ivester, MPA, CMA(AAMA), CLS(NCA)
North Georgia Technical College
Clarkesville, GA

Josephine Jackyra, CMA
The Technical Institute of Camden County
Sicklerville, NJ

Deborah Jones, BS, MA
High-Tech Institute
Phoenix, AZ

Karl A. Kahley, CHE, BS
Instructor, Medical Assisting
Ogeechee Technical College
Statesboro, GA

Barbara Kalfin Kalish
City College, Palm Beach Community College
Ft Lauderdale, FL

Cheri D. Keenan, MA Instructor, EMT-B
Remington College
Garland, TX

Barbara E. Kennedy, RN, CPhT
Blair College
Colorado Springs, CO

Tammy C. Killough, RN, BSN
Texas Careers Vocational Nursing Program Director
San Antonio, TX

Jimmy Kinney, AAS
Virginia College at Huntsville
Huntsville, AL

Karen A. Kittle, CMA, CPT, CHUC
Oakland Community College
Waterford, MI

Diane M. Klieger, RN, MBA, CMA
Pinellas Technical Education Centers
St. Petersburg, FL

Mary E. Larsen, CMT, RMA
Academy of Professional Careers
Nampa, ID

Nancy L. Last, RN
Eagle Gate College
Murray, UT

Holly Roth Levine, NCICS, NCRMA, BA, BSN, RN
Keiser College
West Palm Beach, FL

Christine Malone, BS
Everett Community College
Everett, WA

Janice Manning
Baker College
Jackson, MI

Loretta Mattio-Hamilton, AS, CMA, RPT, CCA, NCICS
Herzing College
Kenner, LA

Gayle Mazzocco, BSN, RN, CMA
Oakland Community College
Waterford, MI

Patti McCormick, RN, PHD
President, Institute of Holistic Leadership
Dayton, OH

Heidi M. McLean, CMA, RMA, BS, RPT, CAHI
Anne Arundel Community College
Arnold, MD

Stephanie R. McGahee, AATH
Augusta Technical College
Thomson, GA

Tanya Mercer, BS, RN, RMA
KAPLAN Higher Education Corporation
Roswell, GA

Sandra J. Metzger, RN, BSN, MS. Ed
Red Rocks Community College
Lakewood, CO

Joyce A. Minton, BS, CMA, RMA
Wilkes Community College
Wilkesboro, NC

Grace Moodt, RN, BSN
Wallace Community College
Dothan, AL

Sherry L. Mulhollen, BS, CMA
Elmira Business Institute
Elmira, NY

Deborah M. Mullen, CPC, NCMA
Sanford Brown Institute
Atlanta, GA

Michael Murphy, CMA
Berdan Institute @ The Summit Medical Group
Union, NJ

Lisa S. Nagle, CMA, BS.Ed,
Augusta Technicial College
Augusta, GA

Peggy Newton, BSN, RN
Galen Health Institute
Louisville, KY

Brigitte Niedzwiecki, RN, MSN
Chippewa Valley Technical College
Eau Claire, WI

Thomas E. O'Brien, MBA, BBA, AS, CCT
Central Florida Institute
Palm Harbor, FL

Linda Oliver, MA
Vista Adult School
Vista, CA

Linda L. Oprean, BSN
ACT College
Manassas, VA

Holly J. Paul, MSN, FNP
Baker College of Jackson
Jackson, MI

Shirley Perkins, MD, BSE
Everest College
Dallas, TX

Kristina Perry, BPA
Heritage College
Las Vegas, NV

James H. Phillips, BS, CMA, RMA
Central Florida College
Winter Park, FL

Carol Putkamer, RHIA, MS
Alpena Community College
Alpena, MI

Mary Rahr, MS, RN, CMA-C
Northeast Wisconsin Technical College
Green Bay, WI

David Rice, AA, BA, MA
Career College of Northern Nevada
Reno, NV

Dana M. Roessler, RN, BSN
Southeastern Technical College
Glennville, GA

Cindy Rosburg, MA
Wisconsin Indian Technical College
New Richmond, WI

Deborah D. Rossi, MA, CMA
Community College of Philadelphia
Philadelphia, PA

Donna Rust, BA
American Commercial College
Wichita Falls, TX

Ona Schulz, CMA
Lake Washington Technical College
Kirkland, WA

Amy E. Semenchuk, RN, BSN
Rockford Business College
Rockford, IL

David Lee Sessoms, Jr. M.Ed., CMA
Miller-Motte Technical College
Cary, NC

Susan Shorey, BA, MA
Valley Career College
El Cajon, CA

Lynn G. Slack, BS
ICM School of Business and Medical Careers
Pittsburgh, PA

Patricia L. Slusher, MT(ASCP), CMA
Ivy Tech State College
Kokomo, IN

Deborah H. Smith, RN, CNOR
Southeastern Technical College
Vidalia, GA

Kristi Sopp, AA
MTI College
Sacramento, CA

Nona K. Stinemetz, Practical Nurse
Vatterott College
Des Moines, IA

Patricia Ann Stoddard, MS, RT(R), MT, CMA
Western Business College
Vancouver, WA

Sylvia Taylor, BS, CMA, CPC-A
Cleveland State Community College
Cleveland, TN

Cynthia H. Thompson, RN, MA
Davenport University
Bay City, MI

Geiselle Thompson, M. Div.
The Learning Curve Plus
Cary, NC

Barbara Tietsort, M. Ed.
University of Cincinnati, Raymond Walters
Cincinnati, OH

Karen A. Trompke, RN
Virginia College at Pensacola
Pensacola, FL

Marilyn M. Turner, RN, CMA
Ogeechee Technical College
Statesboro, GA

L. Joleen VanBibber, AS
Davis Applied Technology College
Kaysville, UT

Lynette M. Veach, AAS
Columbus State Community College
Columbus, OH 43215

Antonio C. Wallace, BS
Sanford Brown Institute
Atlanta, GA

Jim Wallace, MHSA
Maric College
Los Angeles, CA

Denise Wallen, CPC
Academy of Professional Careers
Boise, ID

Mary Jo Whitacre, MSN, RN
Lord Fairfax Community College
Middletown, VA

Donna R. Williams, LPN, RMA
Tennessee Technology Center
Knoxville, TN

Marsha Lynn Wilson, BS, MS (ABT)
Clarian Health Sciences Education Center
Indianapolis, IN

Linda V. Wirt, CMA
Cecil Community College
North East, MD

Dr. MaryAnn Woods, PhD, RN
Prof. Emeritus,
Fresno City College
Fresno, CA 93741

Bettie Wright, MBA, CMA
Umpqua Community College
Roseburg, OR

Mark D. Young, DMD, BS
West Kentucky Community and Technical College
Paducah, KY

Cynthia M. Zumbrun, MEd, RHIT, CCS-P
Allegany College of Maryland
Cumberland, MD

Instructions for the Procedure Competency Checklists

General Instructions

Review and practice the correct performance of each procedure prior to attempting the procedure. The rationales for all critical steps are given in the performance guidelines within your textbook. Review these steps and rationales carefully before beginning the procedure. As you become more proficient in the procedure, you should perform the procedure without guidance from the textbook or the reviewer. In any procedure, certain steps are considered to be more "important" than others. These steps are referred to as **critical steps.** If any of these steps are missed or performed incorrectly, you should continue to practice the procedure to perfect the technique. Steps with an * are considered critical steps.

Scoring System

To score each step, use the following scoring system:
1 = poor, 2 = fair, 3 = good, 4 = excellent

A minimum score of at least a 3 must be achieved on **each** step to achieve successful completion of the technique. Calculate the final score by dividing the total number of points achieved by the total possible points listed at the top of the grading table and multiply by 100. For example, if the total possible score is 40 (10×4) and a score of 36 was achieved it would be $36/40 \times 100$ or 90. Remember that steps with an * are considered **critical steps.** If a critical step is not done correctly, you will be considered unsuccessful in completing the procedure during that attempt.

The procedure templates allow for three practice attempts and a final performance. The three practice attempts may be judged by other students or lab assistants. There are areas available for observer comments so that you may improve your technique with each procedure attempt. The final performance should be assessed by the instructor or a designated lab assistant.

Name ______________________________ Class ____________________ Date ____________

CHAPTER 1

The Profession of Medical Assisting

Review

Vocabulary Review

True or False

Decide whether each statement is true or false. In the space at the left, write T *for* true *or* F *for* false. *On the lines provided, rewrite the false statements to make them true.*

_______ 1. A practitioner is someone who practices a profession.

____

_______ 2. The American Association of Medical Assistants works to raise standards of medical assisting to a professional level.

____

_______ 3. You do not need to pass the American Medical Technologists certification examination to qualify as a Registered Medical Assistant (RMA).

____

_______ 4. A Certified Medical Assistant (CMA) credential is automatically renewed.

____

_______ 5. Accreditation is the process by which programs are officially authorized.

____

_______ 6. Externships are voluntary in accredited schools.

____

_______ 7. When a medical assistant is able to perform many duties in the office, the medical assistant is considered to be cross-trained.

____

_______ 8. The Medical Assistant Role Delineation Chart provides the basis for education and evaluation in the medical assistant field.

____

Name ______________________________ Class ____________________ Date ____________

Content Review

Multiple Choice

In the space provided, write the letter of the choice that best completes each statement or answers each question.

_______ **1.** To receive certification or registration as a medical assistant, you must
- **A.** graduate from an approved program with a bachelor's degree in medical assisting.
- **B.** become a member of the American Association of Medical Assistants (AAMA) or American Medical Technologists (AMT).
- **C.** graduate from an approved medical assistant program and pass the AAMA or AMT examination.
- **D.** pass the AAMA or AMT examination.
- **E.** become a multiskilled professional.

_______ **2.** Formal training programs in medical assisting
- **A.** are offered only at 2-year colleges.
- **B.** can be replaced by on-the-job training.
- **C.** must be approved by the AAMA or AMT.
- **D.** last 1 to 2 years and award a certificate, diploma, or associate degree.

_______ **3.** Being able to change your schedule and meet your employer's needs is considered
- **A.** self-motivation.
- **B.** flexibility.
- **C.** attitude.
- **D.** willingness to learn.
- **E.** being multiskilled.

_______ **4.** The definition of diplomacy is
- **A.** taking a stand about your beliefs and morals.
- **B.** a positive attitude.
- **C.** holding yourself to high standards.
- **D.** being able to communicate without offending anyone.

_______ **5.** A person with integrity
- **A.** maintains high standards.
- **B.** is honest and dependable.
- **C.** is reliable.
- **D.** is all of the above.

Sentence Completion

In the space provided, write the word or phrase that best completes each sentence.

6. Medical assisting is a(n) _______ allied health profession because practitioners can handle many different duties.

7. Using _______ means evaluating circumstances, solving problems, and taking action.

8. _______ is the ability to put yourself in someone else's shoes.

9. Effective _______ involves careful listening, observing, speaking, and writing.

10. Helping the receptionist prepare the next day's charts is an example of _______.

6. ______________________

7. ______________________

8. ______________________

9. ______________________

10. ______________________

Name ______________________ Class ______________ Date __________

11. It is important that a medical assistant's appearance reflects a _______. 11. ______________

12. Medical assistants should always conduct themselves in a _______. 12. ______________

13. Reporting a mistake to a physician is an example of _______ . 13. ______________

14. Being able to understand both sides of any situation is an example of _______. 14. ______________

Short Answer

Write the answer to each question on the lines provided.

15. List three administrative duties performed by a medical assistant.

16. List three clinical duties performed by a medical assistant.

17. List three laboratory duties performed by a medical assistant.

18. Describe ethical behavior for medical assistants.

19. What is the scope of practice?

20. List three areas of competence from the Medical Assistant Role Delineation Chart.

21. To ensure HIPAA compliance, what is the best way to dispose of paper in the medical office?

22. List three reasons why credentialing is important for a medical assistant's entry and advancement in the medical environment.

23. Why is a good attitude important in a medical environment?

24. What is tact?

25. Why would body piercing affect your ability to obtain a job?

26. Why is continuing education important for medical assistants?

27. What is a managed care organization?

28. What are three certification exams offered by the National Healthcare Association that medical assistants can take?

Critical Thinking

Write the answer to each question on the lines provided.

1. Why is a medical assistant's willingness to work as a team member so important to a medical facility?

Name ______________________ Class ______________ Date ____________

2. How does self-motivation apply to your studies?

3. Why would someone who does not pay attention to details be poorly suited for a career as a medical assistant?

4. Why is your appearance so important in health care?

5. How can you determine if your attitude is what is required of a medical assistant?

6. Give one example of integrity in the medical office.

Application

Follow the directions for the application.

1. **Appropriate Work Dress**

   Work with a partner to collect information on appropriate dress for work in a medical office.

   a. Collect and request a collection of uniform catalogs from the Internet. Here are two popular sites: www.Jascouniform.com and www.Allheart.com.

   b. Clip pictures of uniforms that you like and complete the "perfect" medical wardrobe.

   c. Research and find pictures of clothing and accessories that are not suitable for the medical profession.

   d. Make a collage of the two types of clothing—appropriate and inappropriate—and discuss with the class and instructor.

2. **Personal Qualifications of Medical Assistants**

   Make a list of the 16 personal qualifications of medical assistants and write a sentence or two describing how these qualifications enhance quality patient care and contribute to professional relationships with the allied health team in the medical facility. Facilitate a class discussion about your statements.

Name ____________________ Class ____________ Date __________

Case Studies

Write your response to each case study on the lines provided.

Case 1

It is a very busy Monday and you only have one appointment slot open. One patient calls and complains of flu-like symptoms and is feeling generally unwell. She would like an appointment today. A second patient calls complaining of vomiting and diarrhea and has been unable to eat for 24 hours. He would like to come in today but will wait until tomorrow. The third patient is a college student and forgot he needs a physical in order to be allowed to play basketball. He is in town for two days. An appointment today would fit in well with his schedule. Which patient should be given the appointment slot? If you cannot determine who should get the one available appointment, who should you consult regarding this decision?

____

____

____

Case 2

Suppose you work as a medical assistant in a cardiologist's office. In your spare time, you read about new advances in heart medications. Even though only the doctor can prescribe medications, how might this knowledge help you in your job?

____

____

____

Case 3

You are involved in a group interview. The medical assistant that you are interviewing is credentialed and has a lot of good experience. She seems pleasant, but you notice that she has a "Right to Life" tattoo on her forearm, a tongue ring, and facial piercings. How do you think your elderly patients and female patients will perceive her? How might the physician perceive her?

____

____

____

Case 4

You are working with another medical assistant and you notice that she is recording vital statistics in the chart but is not actually taking measurements. What should you do? How does ethical behavior apply here?

____

____

____

Name ______________________ Class ______________ Date ____________

CHAPTER 2

Types of Medical Practice

Review

Vocabulary Review

Matching

Match the key terms in the right column with the definitions in the left column by placing the letter of each correct answer in the space provided.

_____ **1.** A physician who is a generalist and treats all types and ages of patients

_____ **2.** A physician who diagnoses and treats diseases of the nervous system

_____ **3.** A physician who specializes in the diagnosis and treatment of diseases of the heart and blood vessels

_____ **4.** To assess immediate medical needs of a patient

_____ **5.** A physician who specializes in treating patients with cancer

_____ **6.** A physician who diagnoses and treats diseases and disorders of the muscles and bones

_____ **7.** A physician who diagnoses and treats problems related to the internal organs

_____ **8.** A physician who studies, diagnoses, and treats kidney disease

_____ **9.** A physician who diagnoses and treats disorders of the gastrointestinal tract

_____ **10.** A physician who diagnoses and treats disorders of the endocrine system

_____ **11.** A physician who studies disease and the changes it produces in the cells, fluids, and processes of the entire body

_____ **12.** A physician who diagnoses and treats diseases of the kidney, bladder, and urinary system

_____ **13.** A physician who provides routine physical care of the female reproductive system

_____ **14.** A physician who performs the reconstruction, correction, or improvement of body structures

_____ **15.** A specialist who diagnoses and treats diseases and disorders with physical therapy

_____ **16.** A physician who uses a "whole person" approach to health care

a. cardiologist
b. endocrinologist
c. family practitioner
d. gastroenterologist
e. gynecologist
f. internist
g. nephrologist
h. neurologist
i. oncologist
j. orthopedist
k. pathologist
l. physiatrist
m. plastic surgeon
n. triage
o. urologist
p. physician assistant
q. acupuncturist
r. massage therapist
s. chiropractor
t. doctor of osteopathy

S 17. A specialist who treats patients who are ill or in pain without using drugs or surgery

R 18. A specialist who uses pressure, kneading, stroking, vibration, and tapping to promote muscle and full-body relaxation

Q 19. A specialist who uses a Chinese theory based on beliefs of how the body works

P 20. A health-care provider who practices medicine under the supervision of a physician

True or False

Decide whether each statement is true or false. In the space at the left, write T *for* true *or* F *for* false. *On the lines provided, rewrite the false statements to make them true.*

______ **21.** An endocrinologist diagnoses and treats physical reactions to substances such as dust and pollen.

______ **22.** An otorhinolaryngologist diagnoses and treats illnesses of the ear, nose, and throat.

______ **23.** A neurologist uses medical instruments to correct deformities and treat external and internal injuries or disease.

______ **24.** A nephrologist uses medications to cause patients to lose sensation during surgery.

______ **25.** A doctor of osteopathy holds the title DO and focuses attention on the musculoskeletal system.

______ **26.** A gynecologist specializes in the treatment of problems and diseases of older adults.

______ **27.** A gastroenterologist specializes in the diagnosis and treatment of diseases of the skin, hair, and nails.

______ **28.** A pediatrician diagnoses and treats childhood diseases.

______ **29.** A physiatrist specializes in taking and reading x-rays.

______ **30.** A typical treatment plan for a chiropractor involves exercise programs, manual treatments, and anti-inflammatory medications.

______ **31.** Massage therapists use techniques that increase circulation, remove waste products from injured tissues, and bring fresh blood and nutrients to areas of the body to speed healing.

______ **32.** Physician assistants are qualified to diagnose medical problems, order lab tests, and carry out treatment plans.

Name ______________________ Class ______________ Date ____________

Content Review

Multiple Choice

In the space provided, write the letter of the choice that best completes each statement or answers each question.

__B__ **1.** A physician who wishes to specialize in a particular branch of medicine
- **A.** must complete 1 additional year of residency in that specialty.
- **B.** must complete an additional 2 to 6 years of residency in that specialty.
- **C.** must complete a bachelor's degree in that specialty.
- **D.** may do so without any additional education.

__B__ **2.** Radiology is the branch of medical science that
- **A.** is a subspecialty of neurology.
- **B.** uses x-rays and radioactive substances to diagnose and treat disease.
- **C.** provides the scientific foundation for all medical practice.
- **D.** studies and records the electrical activity of the brain.
- **E.** introduces a small amount of radioactive substance into the body.

__D__ **3.** A professional who has studied the chemical and physical qualities of drugs and dispenses such medication to the public is a
- **A.** nurse practitioner.
- **B.** pharmacy technician.
- **C.** medical technologist.
- **D.** pharmacist.

__C__ **4.** Which of the following takes health histories, performs physical exams, conducts screening tests, and educates patients and families about disease prevention?
- **A.** Occupational therapist
- **B.** Associate degree nurse
- **C.** Independent nurse practitioner
- **D.** Licensed practical nurse
- **E.** Clinical laboratory technician

__A__ **5.** A health-care professional who works under the direction of a physician and manages medical emergencies that occur away from the medical setting is a(n)
- **A.** emergency medical technician.
- **B.** surgeon's assistant.
- **C.** radiation therapy technologist.
- **D.** pathologist's assistant.

Sentence Completion

In the space provided, write the word or phrase that best completes each sentence.

6. A physician who is a generalist and treats all types of patients is referred to as a(n) _______ by insurance companies.

7. Using therapy with electricity, heat, cold, ultrasound, massage, and exercise, a(n) _______ helps restore physical function and relieve pain following disease or injury.

8. _______ are allied health professionals trained to draw blood for diagnostic laboratory testing.

6. primary care physician
7. fsical therapys or fsical therapist assistant
8. phlebotomists.

Name ______________________ Class ______________ Date __________

9. A(n) _______works with emotionally disturbed and mentally retarded patients and assists the psychiatric team.

10. A(n) _______ translates a physician's directions about patient treatments into comprehensive, typed records.

11. While transferring patients to the hospital, a(n) _______ records, documents, and radios the patient's condition to the physician, describing how the injury occurred.

12. One medical assistant specialty, that of the _______, involves assisting the pediatrician in administrative and clinical duties.

13. Working under the supervision of a physician and a respiratory therapist, a(n) _______ performs procedures such as artificial ventilation.

14. Working under the supervision of a medical technologist, a certified _______ performs routine procedures in bacteriology, chemistry, hematology, parasitology, serology, and urinalysis.

15. Membership in a(n) _______, such as the American Medical Technologists, enables one to get involved in relevant issues and activities.

16. _______ introduces a small amount of radioactive substance into the body and forms an image by detecting radiation as it leaves the body.

9. Mental helth technician / psychiatry counselor
10. Medical transcriptions
11. EMT Emergancia Medical
12. pediatric Medical Assistant
13. Respiratory therapy technician
14. laboratory Assistant.
15. Professional Association
16. Nuclear Medicine.

Short Answer

Write the answer to each question on the lines provided.

17. What is the purpose of a residency?

____

____

____

18. When might a family practitioner send a patient to a specialist?

____

____

____

19. What is the difference between a gynecologist and an obstetrician/gynecologist?

____

____

____

20. What is the difference between an ophthalmologist and an optometrist?

____

____

____

Name ________________________ Class ________________ Date ____________

21. Discuss the differences in the training and job duties of an LPN and a medical assistant.

22. What are three duties of a medical administrative assistant?

23. In what types of settings can phlebotomists work?

24. Explain the difference between a licensed practical nurse (LPN) and a registered nurse (RN).

25. What is osteopathic manipulative medicine?

26. Describe the manual treatments and diagnostic testing that chiropractors use to treat patients.

27. Describe the principles of acupuncture.

28. Describe two conditions that a proctologist would treat.

Name ______________________ Class ______________ Date __________

Critical Thinking

Write the answer to each question on the lines provided.

1. What are the benefits of learning about the medical specialties and subspecialties?

2. What are the differences between medical assistants and physician assistants?

3. Compare the education and qualifications of an MD and a DO, describing the differences in their training and approach to patient care.

4. Discuss how a medical assistant may interact with other health-care professionals or specialists.

5. Compare DOs and chiropractors. How are their practices different? How are they similar or the same?

6. Why are patients referred to specialty physicians?

APPLICATION

Follow the directions for each application.

1. **Certification**

   Using the Internet, research the AMT, the AAMA, and the National Healthcare Association. Select two certifications that you would like to complete upon graduation. Request informational brochures and applications, and distribute them to the class.

2. Specialist Interview

As a follow-up to studying the various specialties, choose a medical specialist to interview and report on your findings.

a. Review the specialty careers described in the text. Select one.

b. Check the telephone book or other sources to find specialists in the area you chose. Write down the names and phone numbers of three to five specialists.

c. Call the offices of the specialists until you find a specialist who will grant you a 15- to 30-minute interview. Make an appointment for the interview.

d. Prepare a list of six to ten interview questions. Include questions that address the type and amount of education required, responsibilities and duties, and advantages and disadvantages of the specialty. Also include a question about what personal skills are required. Conclude by asking for advice that the specialist can offer someone interested in pursuing the specialty.

e. Dress professionally for the interview. Take your list of questions, a pen, and a pad to the interview.

f. Conduct the interview, keeping it within the time limit you promised. Thank the specialist for her time.

g. Send a thank-you note to the specialist within a week of the interview.

h. Share your findings with your classmates through a format of your choice: oral presentation, written report, or interview "question and answer" news article.

3. Medical Specialties

Research the Internet for specialties in which a medical assistant may be employed. Research the credentials needed and the experience required for the job. Then find a position within the specialty and research what duties are performed by the position and how you may gain those skills. Report your findings to the class.

Case Studies

Write your response to each case study on the lines provided.

Case 1

You are currently working for an internist who treats a variety of skin conditions, such as acne, eczema, and hives. A patient presents with a small lesion that has not healed in several months. The physician requests that you submit a referral to a dermatologist. Why would this patient seek medical care from a dermatologist instead of being treated by the internist?

____

____

____

Case 2

You are working in an ob/gyn practice. One of your patients confides in you that her husband is suffering from the sexual dysfunction impotence. She would like her husband to seek medical attention for his condition, but she does not know what type of medical specialty treats this condition. What type of specialist should the patient see?

____

____

____

Name ______________________ Class ______________ Date __________

Case 3

You are working in a family practice office. A longtime patient makes an appointment for a diabetes follow-up. She weighs more than 500 pounds and is having difficulty controlling her diabetes as well as problems with general mobility. She asks you what options she has to lose the extra weight. What surgical options might be available to her? Will her insurance pay for weight-control surgery?

____

____

____

Case 4

You are working as a lab assistant in a reference lab. You would like to work as a phlebotomist, but you need certification in phlebotomy as a requirement of the job. How would you research phlebotomy certification? Who should you contact?

____

____

____

Name ______________________ Class ______________ Date ____________

CHAPTER 3

Legal and Ethical Issues in Medical Practice, Including HIPAA

Review

Vocabulary Review

Passage Completion

Study the key terms in the box. Use your textbook to find definitions of terms you do not understand.

abandonment	durable power of attorney	law	negligence
agent	electronic transaction record	law of agency	subpoena
arbitration	ethics	liable	tort
bioethics	felony	living will	treatment, payment, and operations (TPO)
breach of contract	Health Insurance Portability and Accountability Act (HIPAA)	moral values	Uniform Donor Card
civil law		malpractice claims	use
crime		Notice of Privacy Practices	
disclosure			

In the space provided, complete the following passage, using some of the terms from the box. You may change the form of a term to fit the meaning of the sentence.

Medical workers must follow (1) _______ that govern the practice of medicine to prevent patients from filing (2) _______. Patients might charge (3) _______ if a medical worker does not perform an essential action or performs an improper one. A medical worker who stops care without providing an equally qualified substitute can be charged with (4) _______.

Doctors and their patients have an implied contract. A violation of that contract is a(n) (5) _______. If such a violation leads to harm, the violation is called a(n) (6) _______. Some lawsuits go to trial, whereas others are settled through (7) _______. If a case goes to trial, the people involved will receive a(an) (8) _______, requiring their presence in court.

1. ______________________
2. ______________________
3. ______________________
4. ______________________
5. ______________________
6. ______________________
7. ______________________
8. ______________________

Name ______________________ Class ______________________ Date ______________

According to the (9) _______, physicians are responsible, or (10) _______, for everything their employees do. A medical assistant is acting on the physician's behalf and is therefore a(n) (11) _______ of the physician.

Medical assistants often assist patients in completing a(n) (12) _______, which states what type of treatment the patient wishes or does not wish to receive if the patient becomes terminally ill or permanently comatose. The patient may assign a(n) (13) _______ to a person who will make medical decisions if the patient cannot. People who wish to donate one or more organs upon their death complete a legal document called a(n) (14) _______.

In addition to observing medical laws, medical workers must follow a code of (15) _______, which defines general principles of right and wrong. Medical workers may also have to deal with issues in (16) _______ when questions related to medical advances arise.

A(n) (17) _______ is an offense against the state. A(n) (18) _______ is defined as a rule of conduct. (19) _______ is considered a standard of behavior and the concept of right and wrong. (20) _______ serve as a basis for ethical conduct. Practicing medicine without a license is considered a(n) (21) _______. Crimes against the person are considered (22) _______.

HIPAA stands for (23) _______. Under HIPAA, (24) _______ limits the sharing of information within a covered entity, while (25) _______ restricts the sharing of information outside the entity holding the information. HIPAA will allow the provider to share patient information for (26) _______. The document under HIPAA that is the communication of patient rights is called (27) _______. The (28) _______ are the codes and formats used for the exchange of medical data under the HIPAA administrative simplification rule.

9. law agent
10. liable
11. agent
12. living will
13. ______
14. urf
15. Etd.
16. Bioet
17. crimy
18. law.
19. ethics
20. More Values
21. felony
22. civil law.
23. HIPPA
24. use
25. exclosey
26. TPO
27. NPT
28. Electronic

Content Review

Multiple Choice

In the space provided, write the letter of the choice that best completes each statement or answers each question.

__E__ 1. The term *res ipsa loquitur* refers to cases in which

- **A.** the patient has a previously existing condition.
- **B.** the physician abandons the patient.
- **C.** the patient has already filed a lawsuit.
- **D.** the doctor's error was caused by faulty record keeping.
- **E.** the doctor's mistake is clear to everyone.

E 2. If a physician decides to terminate his care of a patient, the physician must
- A. tell the patient face-to-face.
- B. leave a message for the patient on the patient's answering machine.
- C. obtain the patient's consent.
- D. inform the patient's family.
- E. send the patient a certified letter.

D 3. Which of the following is *not* a legal procedure for medical assistants to perform?
- A. Maintaining licenses and accreditation
- B. Recruiting qualified medical assistants for the medical office
- C. Determining needs for documentation and reporting
- D. Diagnosing a condition

A 4. A physician's receptionist asks patients to sign in and list the reason for their visit. This receptionist is violating the patients' right to
- A. confidentiality.
- B. a second opinion.
- C. sue for malpractice.
- D. be seen by the physician in a timely manner.

C 5. While practicing within the context of an implied contract with a patient, the physician is obligated to do all of the following *except*
- A. use due care.
- B. provide complete information and instructions to the patient about diagnoses, options, and methods of treatment.
- C. promise the patient that he or she will recover completely.
- D. stay current regarding all technology and treatments available.

C 6. After disposable sharp equipment has been used, it should be
- A. recapped as soon as possible.
- B. wrapped in its original packaging.
- C. placed in an appropriate container.
- D. broken and placed in a wastepaper basket.

B 7. Crimes such as attempted burglary and disturbing the peace are examples of
- A. felonies.
- B. misdemeanors.
- C. civil law.
- D. intentional crimes.
- E. social crimes.

B 8. If a medical assistant gives a patient an injection after the patient refused the procedure, it could result in a charge of
- A. assault.
- B. battery.
- C. false imprisonment.
- D. *not applicable;* no charge would result because the physician ordered the procedure.

B 9. Preventing a patient from leaving the medical facility after administration of an allergy injection could be seen as
- A. an invasion of privacy.
- B. false imprisonment.
- C. an acceptable practice as long as it was documented in the chart.
- D. malpractice.

Name ______________________ Class ______________________ Date ______________________

a 10. If a patient can prove that she felt "reasonable apprehension of bodily harm," it can result in what type of charge?

A. Defamation of character
B. Battery
C. Assault
D. Negligence
E. Slander

Sentence Completion

In the space provided, write the word or phrase that best completes each sentence.

11. Misfeasance refers to a lawful act that is done ________.
12. The four Ds of negligence are duty, derelict, ________, and damages.
13. The relationship between a doctor and a patient is called an implied ________.
14. Universal Precautions were developed by the Centers for Disease Control and Prevention to protect workers from exposure to ________ pathogens.
15. Damaging a person's reputation by making public statements that are both false and malicious is considered ________.
16. Health-care practitioners who promise patients miracle cures or accept fees from patients while using mystical or spiritual powers to heal is considered ________.
17. A contract that is stated in written or spoken words is considered a(n) ________.
18. Torts that are committed without the intention to cause harm but are committed unreasonably or with a disregard for the consequences are ________.
19. A patient who rolls up her sleeve and offers her arm for an injection is entering into a(n) ________ contract.
20. A document that communicates patient rights under HIPAA is called ________.

11. Incorrect
12. dive Co.
13. contract
14. Blood Born
15. defamation of Caracter
16. ________
17. express contract
18. Intentional
19. ________
20. MPP.

Short Answer

Write the answer to each question on the lines provided.

21. What is the difference between malfeasance and nonfeasance?

____

22. List eight types of personal information that is considered individually identifiable health information under HIPAA.

Name adress Phone number

____

Name ______________________ Class ______________ Date __________

23. What types of protected health information are subject to the Privacy Rule under HIPAA?

past present and future mental help. the mental status.

24. HIPAA allows the provider to share what type of patient health-care information with outside entities?

Care charges don leave staff in the desk all information its Confidentiality

25. List five recommendations under HIPAA to ensure chart security.

26. What are the civil penalties for HIPAA privacy violations?

27. What is authorization under HIPAA?

28. HIPAA allows patient information to be disclosed without authorization in special circumstances. List five entities with whom or situations in which patient information can be disclosed without authorization.

29. Explain what a contract is.

30. List and briefly define the four essential elements of a contract.

31. List the four types of medical practice and provide an advantage of each.

32. How can an office prevent lawsuits?

33. What part of the medical record does the patient own and what part does the physician own?

34. Describe the Federal False Claims Act.

35. How can office equipment compromise confidential medical information?

Critical Thinking

Write the answer to each question on the lines provided.

1. A medical assistant promises a terminally ill patient a cure. Whom can the patient sue, the doctor or the medical assistant? Explain.

2. Do you think the number of bioethical issues will increase or decrease in the future? Why?

3. A physician changes her schedule to be available from 9:00 A.M. until 3:00 P.M. Monday through Friday. Is the physician obligated to schedule evening appointments to accommodate her patients who work during her office hours?

4. How can a medical assistant help prevent lawsuits?

5. How can a medical office safeguard protected health information that is transmitted via fax machines, shared printers, and copiers?

____

____

____

Application

Follow the directions for the application.

Writing a Letter of Withdrawal

Work with two partners. Take turns being a medical assistant, a doctor, and an evaluator. Assume that the doctor has asked the medical assistant to write a letter of withdrawal to a patient.

a. The doctor should explain to the medical assistant what the problem with the patient is and why he has decided to withdraw from the case. The medical assistant should take notes and ask questions as necessary.

b. The medical assistant should then write the letter for the doctor. She should make clear the doctor's reason for withdrawing from the case. She should also include the doctor's recommendation that the patient seek medical care from another doctor as soon as possible.

c. After the foregoing tasks have been completed, the evaluator should critique the letter, keeping in mind the following questions: Does the letter include the doctor's reason for withdrawing from the case? Does the letter include the doctor's recommendation that the patient seek medical care elsewhere? Is the letter free of spelling, punctuation, and grammatical errors? Does it follow a business letter format?

d. The medical assistant and the doctor should discuss the evaluator's comments, noting the strengths and weaknesses of the letter.

e. Exchange roles and repeat the procedure with another student as a doctor who wishes to terminate care of a patient for a different reason.

f. Exchange roles again so that each member of the team has the opportunity to role-play the medical assistant, the doctor, and the evaluator.

Case Studies

Write your response to each case study on the lines provided.

Case 1

A patient has a sexually transmitted disease but does not want you or the doctor to contact any former sex partners. The doctor has asked you to handle this case. How much can you do to make sure these people are notified?

____

____

____

Name ______________________ Class ______________ Date __________

Case 2

A doctor is about to leave on a special family vacation for two months. A new patient comes to the office with a collection of unusual symptoms that do not seem to be serious. The doctor tells the patient to make another appointment for after his return from vacation so that he can order some tests. What kind of lawsuit is the doctor risking? What should the doctor do instead?

____

____

____

Case 3

You work in a large medical office with three other medical assistants. One of the other assistants discusses her patients with you during your lunch break together. What, if anything, has the medical assistant done wrong? What should you do about it?

____

____

____

Case 4

As you walk through the waiting room, a crying woman stops you. Her 14-year-old daughter is in an examining room. The daughter insisted on coming to the doctor but would not tell her mother why. The mother is afraid her daughter is pregnant or has contracted a sexually transmitted disease. What should you say to the mother?

____

____

____

Name ______________________________ Class ____________________ Date ____________

CHAPTER 4

Communication with Patients, Families, and Coworkers

REVIEW

Vocabulary Review

True or False

Decide whether each statement is true or false. In the space at the left, write T *for true or* F *for false. On the lines provided, rewrite the false statements to make them true.*

_______ **1.** Passive listening does not require a response.

____

_______ **2.** Active listening involves two-way communication in which the listener gives feedback or asks questions.

____

_______ **3.** Empathy is the process of feeling sorry for someone.

____

_______ **4.** An aggressive person tries to impose his position on others or tries to manipulate them.

____

_______ **5.** Rapport is a conflictive and argumentative relationship.

____

_______ **6.** Conflict in the workplace arises when two or more coworkers have the same opinions or ideas.

____

_______ **7.** An assertive person has low self-esteem.

____

_______ **8.** Sitting in a chair with your arms crossed is described as having a closed posture.

____

_______ **9.** Personal space is an area that is approximately 4 feet around a person.

____

_______ **10.** Feedback is a verbal or nonverbal response from a patient that she understood what has been communicated.

____

_______ **11.** The manner in which a person interacts with people is referred to as interpersonal skills.

____

_______ **12.** Patients will see a medical assistant as standoffish and reserved when he portrays an open posture.

____

Name ________________ Class ________________ Date ________________

Matching

Match the key terms in the right column with the definitions in the left column by placing the letter of each correct answer in the space provided.

_______ **13.** "You appear tense today."

_______ **14.** "Please, go on."

_______ **15.** Allowing the patient time to think without pressure.

_______ **16.** "I follow what you said."

_______ **17.** "Hi, Mr. Smith. Florida sure agrees with you."

_______ **18.** "Can I help you with your shoes, Mrs. Adams?"

_______ **19.** "Is there something you would like to talk about?"

_______ **20.** "So, you are here today because of your swollen ankles and dizziness?"

_______ **21.** "Describe your level of pain on a scale from one to five, with five being the most severe."

_______ **22.** "Tell me when you feel anxious."

_______ **23.** "So what you are saying is that you feel the most pressure when you exercise?"

_______ **24.** Patient states: "Do you think this is serious enough to discuss with the doctor?" Medical assistant replies: "Do you think it is?"

_______ **25.** "Your granddaughter's first birthday sounded wonderful. Now tell me more about your headaches."

_______ **26.** "You're visiting the doctor today regarding a cough. How long have you been coughing?"

a. acceptance
b. offering self
c. making observations
d. reflecting
e. clarifying
f. exploring
g. offering general leads
h. giving broad openings
i. mirroring
j. recognizing
k. silence
l. summarizing
m. encouraging communication
n. focusing

Content Review

Multiple Choice

In the space provided, write the letter of the choice that best completes each statement or answers each question.

_______ **1.** Noise is anything that
A. helps the patient give feedback.
B. is a part of verbal communication.
C. interferes with the communication process.
D. is part of a communication circle.

_______ **2.** Positive communication with patients may involve
A. getting them to limit their questions to save time.
B. being attentive and encouraging them to ask questions.
C. telling patients who ask questions that their concerns are foolish.
D. allowing them to act on angry or abusive feelings.

_______ **3.** Which of the following is an example of negative communication?
A. Maintaining eye contact
B. Displaying open posture
C. Listening carefully
D. Asking questions
E. Mumbling

Name ______________________________ Class ____________________ Date ____________

_______ **4.** Which of the following is *not* a communication skill?

A. Active listening
B. Anxiety
C. Empathy
D. Assertiveness

_______ **5.** When interacting with patients of other cultures or ethnic groups,

A. assume that they have the same attitude toward modern medicine that you have.
B. never involve other family members.
C. never try to speak their language.
D. never allow yourself to make value judgments.
E. assume that modesty is not essential.

_______ **6.** Which of the following is not a deficiency need as defined by Abraham Maslow?

A. Safety
B. Love
C. Esteem
D. Physiological needs
E. Empathy

_______ **7.** The most effective manner in which to deal with an angry patient is to

A. remind the patient that you are an educated medical assistant.
B. defend the medical facility to the patient.
C. walk away because a medical assistant should not put up with this behavior.
D. demonstrate your sincerity and respect by remaining calm.
E. All of the above.

_______ **8.** The culture that views sexual segregation as important is

A. Hispanic
B. Asian
C. Middle Eastern
D. African American
E. American Indian

_______ **9.** According to Erikson, the life stage that exposes children to people other than their immediate family is

A. Stage I.
B. Stage V.
C. Stage III.
D. Stage IV.
E. Stage II.

_______ **10.** When a teenager begins to smoke at a young age because his peers are doing it, the child is most likely experiencing

A. autonomy.
B. ego identity.
C. role confusion.
D. inferiority.
E. isolation.

Name ________________ Class ________________ Date ________________

Sentence Completion

In the space provided, write the word or phrase that best completes each sentence.

11. A communication circle involves a message, a source, and a(n) _______. **11.** ________________

12. Being _______ when communicating with patients shows them that you, the doctors, and other staff members care about them and their feelings. **12.** ________________

13. Your _______, which is the way you hold or move parts of your body, can send strong nonverbal messages. **13.** ________________

14. If a patient leans back or turns her head away when you lean forward, you may be invading her _______. **14.** ________________

15. The _______ syndrome refers to the anxiety that some patients feel in a doctor's office or other health-care setting. **15.** ________________

16. Positive communication with superiors involves keeping them informed, asking questions, minimizing interruptions, and showing _______. **16.** ________________

17. A(n) _______ manual is a key written communication tool that covers all office policies and clinical procedures in the medical office. **17.** ________________

18. Explaining procedures to patients, expediting insurance referral requests, and creating a warm and reassuring environment are all examples of _______ in the physician office. **18.** ________________

19. _______, a well-known behaviorist, developed a human behavior model that states that human beings are motivated by unsatisfied needs. **19.** ________________

20. A condition that results from prolonged periods of stress without relief is called _______. **20.** ________________

21. A world-renowned authority in death and dying, _______ developed a model of behavior that an individual will experience on learning of his condition. These behaviors are referred to as the stages of dying or the stages of grief. **21.** ________________

Short Answer

Write the answer to each question on the lines provided.

22. What are three other examples of negative communication?

____

____

____

23. List the life stages per Erik Erikson and discuss the expected development traits of each.

____

____

____

Name ______________________ Class ______________ Date __________

24. What is the difference between a stereotype and a generalization of different cultures?

25. What are three means of establishing good communication with a patient who is visually impaired?

26. What are three things you can do to improve communication with a hearing-impaired patient?

27. List four tips for communicating clearly with elderly patients.

28. Describe three things you might do when dealing with very young patients.

29. What are three rules for establishing positive communication with coworkers?

30. Describe the importance of researching the community resources available in your area.

31. List Elisabeth Kübler-Ross's five stages of death and dying and briefly describe them.

Critical Thinking

Write the answer to each question on the lines provided.

1. How does a person's body language convey his true feelings even when his words say otherwise?

2. Explain why learning developmental life span models can help you communicate with patients.

____

____

____

3. Suppose a new medical office does not yet have a policy and procedures manual. What kinds of problems might arise?

____

____

____

4. What therapeutic communication techniques can a medical assistant use when caring for an elderly patient? What defense mechanisms might elderly patients use?

____

____

____

5. Explain how Elisabeth Kübler-Ross's model of the stages of death and dying can help both the families of terminally ill patients and the patients themselves.

____

____

____

6. From the statements by the medical assistant in each scenario listed below, determine which statements are assertive and which are aggressive. Rewrite the aggressive statements to make them assertive.

A. A new patient to your office has begun taking antidepressants. When asking the patient about the new medication, you discover that the patient is only taking the medication when she feels anxious. You respond by saying, "Do you really expect to feel better when you are not following the physician's directions?"

____

____

____

B. A patient has a billing question on a statement that he received recently. You respond, "Let me find the appropriate person to answer the question for you."

____

____

____

C. A coworker uses a profane word by the reception window. You respond by telling her, "You're nasty."

____

____

____

D. Your physician is in her office reviewing lab results when you burst in the room and say, "I have to talk to you now regarding my vacation."

____

____

____

E. You are receiving your annual performance review by your supervisor and you don't agree on several of the improvement items. You respond by saying, "What do you know? You're not a clinical expert."

____

____

____

F. A patient is yelling at you over the telephone and is using profanity with you. You respond by saying, "Please stop cursing at me and let's solve this problem together."

____

____

____

Application

Follow the directions for each application.

1. Policy and Procedures Manual: Writing Policies

A. Working in groups of three or four, write and develop policies for classroom etiquette, such as attendance, cell phone policy, dress code, homework, and testing policies. For each policy, write a consequence if the policy is violated.

B. In the same groups, write and develop policies regarding laboratory procedures. Some examples include disposing of biohazardous waste procedures, removing contaminated gloves, and procedures for laboratory table disinfection. For each procedure, write the purpose of the procedure.

C. Develop a policy and procedures manual using the following steps.

1. Outline or plan for content, such as a table of contents
2. Determine format of the documents
3. Type separate documents for each policy and procedure
4. State date each policy and procedure was adopted for the class
5. Provide name of the writing team, class name, and instructor

Present the policies as a team to the class.

2. Burnout Test

Unmanaged stress can often lead to job burnout in the profession of medical assisting. Answer the following questions *true* or *false* and check your score to see if you are likely to become a victim of burnout.

________ **1.** I feel that the people I know who are in authority are no better than I am.

________ **2.** Once I start a job I have no peace until I finish it.

_______ **3.** I like to tell people exactly what I think.

_______ **4.** Although many people are overly conscious of feelings, I like to deal only with the facts.

_______ **5.** I worry about business and financial matters.

_______ **6.** I often have anxiety about something or someone.

_______ **7.** I sometimes become so preoccupied by a thought that I cannot get it out of my mind.

_______ **8.** I find it difficult to go to bed or to sleep because of the thoughts that bother me.

_______ **9.** I have periods in which I cannot sit or lie down; I need to be doing something.

_______ **10.** My mind is often occupied by thoughts about what I have done wrong or not completed.

_______ **11.** My concentration is not what it used to be.

_______ **12.** My personal appearance is not what it used to be.

_______ **13.** I feel irritated when I see another person's messy desk or cluttered room.

_______ **14.** I am more comfortable in a neat, clean, and orderly room than in a messy one.

_______ **15.** I cannot get through a day or a week without a schedule or a list of jobs to do.

_______ **16.** I believe that the person who works the hardest and longest deserves to get ahead.

_______ **17.** If my job/school/family responsibilities demand(s) more time, I will cut out pleasurable activities to see that they get done.

_______ **18.** My conscience often bothers me about things I have done in the past.

_______ **19.** There are things that I have done that would embarrass me greatly if they become public knowledge.

_______ **20.** I feel uncomfortable unless I get the highest grade.

_______ **21.** It is my view that many people become confused because they do not bother to find out all the facts.

_______ **22.** I frequently feel angry without knowing what or who is bothering me.

_______ **23.** I can't stand to have my checkbook or financial matters out of balance.

_______ **24.** I think that talking about feelings to others is a waste of time.

_______ **25.** There are times when I become preoccupied with washing my hands or keeping things clean.

_______ **26.** I always like to be in control of myself and to know as much as possible about things happening around me.

_______ **27.** I have few or no close friends with whom I share warm feelings openly.

_______ **28.** I feel that the more you can know about future events, the better off you will be.

_______ **29.** There are sins I have committed that I will never live down.

_______ **30.** I always avoid being late to a meeting or an appointment.

_______ **31.** I rarely give up until the job has been completely finished.

_______ **32.** I often expect things out of myself that no one else would ask.

_______ **33.** I sometimes worry about whether I was wrong or made a mistake.

_______ **34.** I would like others to see me as not having any faults.

_______ **35.** The groups and organizations I join have strict rules and regulations.

Name ______________________ Class ______________ Date ____________

Case Studies

Write your response to each case study on the lines provided.

Case 1

A young child is about to receive an injection. He is scared and tearful. You know the injection will hurt slightly, but you decide to put the child's mind at ease by telling him that it won't hurt a bit. Is this the best way to handle the situation? Explain.

Case 2

You are having a problem with a coworker. Both of you have the same job title and often work together to interview and prepare patients. This coworker cuts you off when you speak and contradicts you in front of patients. Her actions are affecting the way patients see you as a professional. How should you handle the situation?

Case 3

A male patient is waiting in the exam room to see the physician. He is seeing the physician for sexual dysfunction. You and several medical assistants are outside his room at the nurse's station and burst into laughter about a comment unrelated to the patient. A few minutes later, the patient leaves. What could have happened to cause the patient to leave? How could this have been avoided?

Case 4

A first-time mother brings her 3-year-old into the pediatrician's office. The child is presenting with behavioral issues regarding potty training. The mother states that the child hides behind furniture instead of using the potty or alerting her of her need to use the bathroom. The mother stated that she has strict consequences when the child has an accident, such as timeouts when an accident occurs. In addition, the older sibling teases the child about accidents. According to Erikson, what is the life stage level for this child and a possible reason for this behavior?

Name ______________________ Class ______________ Date __________

Procedure Competency Checklists

PROCEDURE 4.1 COMMUNICATING WITH THE ANXIOUS PATIENT

Procedure Goal

To use communication and interpersonal skills to calm an anxious patient

Scoring System

To score each step, use the following scoring system:
1 = poor, 2 = fair, 3 = good, 4 = excellent

A minimum score of at least a 3 must be achieved on **each** step to achieve successful completion of the technique. Detailed instructions on the scoring system are found on page x of the Preface.

Materials

None

Procedure

Procedure Steps Total Possible Points - 44 Time Limit: 10 minutes	Practice #1	Practice #2	Practice #3	Final
1. Identify signs of anxiety in the patient.				
2. Acknowledge the patient's anxiety. (Ignoring a patient's anxiety often makes it worse.)*				
3. Identify possible sources of anxiety, such as fear of a procedure or test result, along with supportive resources available to the patient, such as family members and friends. Understanding the source of anxiety in a patient and identifying the supportive resources available can help you communicate with the patient more effectively.				
4. Do what you can to alleviate the patient's physical discomfort. For example, find a calm, quiet place for the patient to wait, a comfortable chair, a drink of water, or access to the bathroom.				
5. Allow ample personal space for conversation. Note: You would normally allow a 1½- to 4-ft distance between yourself and the patient. Adjust this space as necessary.				
6. Create a climate of warmth, acceptance, and trust. a. Recognize and control your own anxiety. Your air of calm can decrease the patient's anxiety. b. Provide reassurance by demonstrating genuine care, respect, and empathy. c. Act confidently and dependably, maintaining truthfulness and confidentiality at all times.				

(continued)

Name ______________________ Class ______________ Date __________

Procedure Steps Total Possible Points - 44 Time Limit: 10 minutes	Practice #1	Practice #2	Practice #3	Final
7. Using the appropriate communication skills, have the patient describe the experience that is causing anxiety, her thoughts about it, and her feelings. Proceeding in this order allows the patient to describe what is causing the anxiety and to clarify her thoughts and feelings about it.* a. Maintain an open posture. b. Maintain eye contact, if culturally appropriate. c. Use active listening skills. d. Listen without interrupting.				
8. Do not belittle the patient's thoughts and feelings. This can cause a breakdown in communication, increase anxiety, and make the patient feel isolated.				
9. Be empathic to the patient's concerns.				
10. Help the patient recognize and cope with the anxiety. a. Provide information to the patient. Patients are often fearful of the unknown. Helping them understand their disease or the procedure they are about to undergo will help decrease their anxiety. b. Suggest coping behaviors, such as deep breathing or other relaxation exercises.				
11. Notify the doctor of the patient's concerns.*				
Total Number of Points Achieved/Final Score				
Initials of Observer:				

Comments and Signatures

Reviewer's comments and signatures:

1. ______________________________

2. ______________________________

3. ______________________________

Instructor's comments:

____

Procedure 4.2 Identifying Community Resources

Procedure Goal

To create a list of useful community resources for patient referrals

Scoring System

To score each step, use the following scoring system:
1 = poor, 2 = fair, 3 = good, 4 = excellent

A minimum score of at least a 3 must be achieved on **each** step to achieve successful completion of the technique. Detailed instructions on the scoring system are found on page x of the Preface.

Name ______________________ Class ______________ Date ________

Materials

Computer with Internet access, phone directory, printer

Procedure

Procedure Steps Total Possible Points - 24 Time Limit: 20 minutes	Practice #1	Practice #2	Practice #3	Final
1. Determine the needs of your medical office and formulate a list of community resources.*				
2. Use the Internet to research the names, addresses, and phone numbers of local resources such as Meals on Wheels, state and federal agencies, home health-care agencies, long-term nursing facilities, mental health agencies, and local charities. Use the phone directory to assist in local agencies as well.				
3. Contact each resource and request information such as business cards and brochures. Some agencies may send a representative to meet with you regarding their services.*				
4. Compile a list of community resources with the proper name, address, phone number, e-mail address, and contact name. Include any information that may be helpful to the office.				
5. Update and add to the information often because outdated information will only frustrate you and your patients, creating even more anxiety.				
6. Post the information in a location where it is readily available.				
Total Number of Points Achieved/Final Score				
Initials of Observer:				

Comments and Signatures

Reviewer's comments and signatures:

1. ____

2. ____

3. ____

Instructor's comments:

____

Name ______________________ Class ______________ Date __________

CHAPTER 5

Using and Maintaining Office Equipment

REVIEW

Vocabulary Review

True or False

Decide whether each statement is true or false. In the space at the left, write T *for true or* F *for false. On the lines provided, rewrite the false statements to make them true.*

_______ 1. When leaving a message on an answering machine, it is important to leave a full and complete message so that anyone who picks up the message can fully understand the reason for the call.

____

_______ 2. A telephone system can be configured so that all incoming calls ring on all the telephones in the office.

____

_______ 3. Medical practices can now use the computer for Internet access and telephone communications.

____

_______ 4. It is not generally necessary to turn off a cell phone when entering a medical practice.

____

_______ 5. The improper or careless use of a patient's answering system or fax machine can be viewed as abusive behavior as determined by HIPAA law.

____

_______ 6. An interactive pager (I-pager) is designed for one-way communication.

____

_______ 7. Faxed material may include protected health information.

____

_______ 8. When a copier jams, the first thing you should do is call technical support.

____

_______ 9. Folding and inserting machines can only be used to fold paper in single folds.

____

_______ 10. According to HIPAA law, when a medical practice sends documents to be shredded by a shredding company, they are no longer responsible for the confidentiality of the information.

____

Name ______________________ Class ______________ Date ________

Matching

Match the key terms in the right column with the definitions in the left column by placing the letter of each correct answer in the space provided.

_______ **11.** Wireless technology

_______ **12.** A practice or behavior that is not indicative of sound medical or fiscal activity

_______ **13.** A small electrical device that gives a signal that someone is trying to reach the carrier

_______ **14.** Paging technology

_______ **15.** A device that scans documents for transmission

_______ **16.** A machine that consists of a meter and a mailing machine

_______ **17.** An alternative to the use of a switchboard and receptionist

_______ **18.** Transforming the spoken word into writing

_______ **19.** A feature of many copiers

_______ **20.** The cancellation of a check

A. A device assigned to a telephone number
B. Postage meter
C. Automated voice response
D. Collating
E. Abuse
F. Transcription
G. Beeper or pager
H. Cell phones
I. Fax machine
J. Voiding

Content Review

Multiple Choice

In the space provided, write the letter of the choice that best completes each statement or answers each question.

_______ **1.** An automated menu answering system

A. answers calls and separates requests into categories.
B. requires answering calls as they come in.
C. does not notify the office when the caller presses the code for a patient emergency.
D. is inappropriate for a medical office.

_______ **2.** Answering services

A. are unreliable.
B. are seldom used by medical practices.
C. can have a direct connection to the doctor's office, answering calls after a certain number of rings.
D. use mechanical voices rather than human voices.
E. are only used in large cities.

_______ **3.** A word processor is helpful to the medical assistant because

A. corrections can be made easily within a document.
B. documents can be stored in memory.
C. the creation of correspondence is a function of the medical assistant.
D. All of the above.

_______ **4.** Which feature is *not* available on a photocopier?

A. Enlarging and reducing the size of a document
B. Collating
C. Folding
D. Stapling

_______ **5.** Which statement is *not* true about fax machines?
- **A.** A fax machine uses a phone line.
- **B.** All fax machines require special thermal paper for printing.
- **C.** Faxes can be received 24 hours a day if the fax machine is turned on.
- **D.** When a fax has been successfully sent, most fax machines print a confirmation message.

_______ **6.** What information can a medical assistant leave on a patient's telephone answering machine?
- **A.** The phone number and name of the medical practice calling
- **B.** Patient information
- **C.** Test results
- **D.** Prescription information

_______ **7.** Interactive pagers
- **A.** are too expensive for widespread use.
- **B.** are difficult to learn how to use.
- **C.** have their own wireless Internet address.
- **D.** are critical to any medical practice.
- **E.** None of the above.

_______ **8.** When the physician determines that a chart can be discarded, you should
- **A.** throw it in the trash.
- **B.** shred it.
- **C.** burn it.
- **D.** keep it for 7 years.
- **E.** store it in a confidential location.

_______ **9.** The postage meter
- **A.** is a convenient and cost-efficient way to apply postage to office correspondence and packages.
- **B.** functions only when there is money in the postal account.
- **C.** automatically senses the weight of a letter or package.
- **D.** A and B only.
- **E.** None of the above.

_______ **10.** A leasing agreement for large office equipment is
- **A.** always preferable to buying.
- **B.** advantageous when you do not have enough money to buy the equipment but you need the service it provides.
- **C.** always less expensive over the long term.
- **D.** never price negotiable.

Sentence Completion

In the space provided, write the word or phrase that best completes each sentence.

11. When the office is closed, many practices use a(n) _______, which will answer the phone, take messages, and communicate them to the doctor on call.

12. When a physician is out of the office, she may carry a(n) _______ so she can be reached if needed.

13. Some fax machines print on specially treated paper, called _______, which reacts to heat and electricity.

11. ____________________

12. ____________________

13. ____________________

Name ________________________________ Class ____________________ Date ____________

14. A(n) _______ is a machine that applies postage to an envelope or package.

15. Medical assistants may be asked to _______ tape-recorded words into written text.

16. A(n) _______ imprints a check with the date, payee's name, and payment amount.

17. The only way to cancel an imprinted check is to _______ it.

18. If the price of the equipment or terms of the sale are not firm, there is room for _______, or bargaining for additional savings or more flexible terms.

19. A(n) _______ tells how a piece of equipment works, what its special features are, and how to troubleshoot problems.

20. Periodically, it will be necessary to conduct an equipment _______, which is a list of a business's equipment.

14. ____________________

15. ____________________

16. ____________________

17. ____________________

18. ____________________

19. ____________________

20. ____________________

Short Answer

Write the answer to each question on the lines provided.

21. Explain how an automated menu telephone system works.

____

____

____

22. What are the benefits of faxing a document?

____

____

____

23. Compare the advantages and disadvantages of an electronic typewriter and a word processor.

____

____

____

24. How might you post packages without a postal scale?

____

____

____

25. Why is using a check writer safer than handwriting a check?

____

____

____

Name ______________________ Class ______________ Date __________

26. List the steps involved in purchasing office equipment.

27. Describe the basic contents of equipment manuals.

28. What does a maintenance contract cover?

29. List three steps in troubleshooting a problem with a piece of equipment.

30. List three pieces of information that many medical practices keep about individual pieces of equipment.

Critical Thinking

Write the answer to each question on the lines provided.

1. How does the almost instantaneous communication of information afforded by today's office equipment influence patient treatment?

2. Automated menus, voice mail, answering machines, and other office communication equipment reduce human contact between health-care workers and patients. What can you do to ensure that patients do not feel cut off by technology?

3. How does office automation affect the staff in a medical office and the care they give patients?

4. What could be a disadvantage of office automation?

____

____

____

5. What might be the advantage of building a relationship with one or two suppliers of office equipment rather than with many?

____

____

____

APPLICATION

Follow the directions for each application.

1. Explaining How to Use Office Equipment

Work with two partners. One should take the role of a medical assistant who has worked in a medical practice for a while and knows how to operate all the office equipment. The second partner should take the role of a new medical assistant who is not familiar with the equipment. The third person should serve as an observer and evaluator.

a. The observer should choose a piece of office equipment, such as a dictation-transcription machine. The experienced medical assistant should then give step-by-step directions on how to use the equipment. The new medical assistant should ask questions to clarify the directions.

b. The evaluator should observe the training session while checking the directions given against those presented in the text.

c. When the training session is complete, the evaluator should provide feedback by citing any omissions or errors in the instructions. All three partners should discuss the effectiveness of the session.

d. Now exchange roles. The new evaluator should choose another piece of equipment to describe in another round of training.

e. Exchange roles again so that each member of the team plays each role at least once. Repeat the activity until all partners achieve confidence in using each piece of equipment.

2. Designing a Fax Cover Sheet

Design a cover sheet to accompany a confidential faxed transmittal from a medical practice.

a. Decide on the type of medical practice. Create the names of the physicians and the address and phone number of the practice.

b. On an 8½- by 11-inch sheet of paper, decide what information to include. Then design your cover sheet.

c. Type the finished cover sheet. Check spelling, grammar, and punctuation.

d. Compare your cover sheet with those of other students. Decide whether you have provided all necessary information. Discuss whether cover sheets should be typed or handwritten and why.

3. Create an Equipment Inventory form

Design an equipment inventory form to list all the equipment in a typical medical practice.

a. Decide on the type of medical practice. Create a form with the name of the practice centered at the top of the form.

b. The form should have columns for the following:

- The name of each piece of equipment
- The date purchased or leased
- An indication of whether each item was purchased or leased
- The price, if purchased
- The leasing arrangement, if leased

c. Use an 8½- by 11-inch sheet of paper and type the finished form.

d. Check spelling, grammar, and punctuation.

e. Compare your form with those of other students and determine the best format.

Case Studies

Write your response to each case study on the lines provided.

Case 1

You are the only one in the office. The physician calls and asks you to get a document over to the laboratory across the street. What can you do?

____

____

____

Case 2

The office manager leaves you a note asking you to fax a document. You place the document in the sending tray of the machine and key in the phone number, but nothing happens. What do you do?

____

____

____

Case 3

In researching a piece of equipment, you find two equally good options. One has a better price and one has a better maintenance agreement. How will you decide which to recommend?

____

____

____

Case 4

You believe a word processor will help you work faster and more efficiently. Your coworkers say the office does not need a word processor. What should you do to convince them?

____

____

____

Name ______________________ Class ______________ Date __________

Procedure Competency Checklists

PROCEDURE 5.1 USING A FACSIMILE (FAX) MACHINE

Procedure Goal

To correctly prepare and send a fax document while following all HIPAA guidelines to guard patient confidentiality

Scoring System

To score each step, use the following scoring system:
1 = poor, 2 = fair, 3 = good, 4 = excellent

A minimum score of at least a 3 must be achieved on **each** step to achieve successful completion of the technique. Detailed instructions on the scoring system are found on page x of the Preface.

Materials

Fax machine, fax line, cover sheet with statement of disclaimer, area code and phone number of fax recipient, document to be faxed, telephone line, and telephone

Procedure

Procedure Steps Total Possible Points - 48 Time Limit: 10 minutes	Practice #1	Practice #2	Practice #3	Final
1. Prepare a **cover sheet,** which provides information about the transmission. Cover sheets can vary in appearance but usually include the name, telephone number, and fax number of the sender and the receiver; the number of pages being transmitted; and the date of the transmission. Preprinted cover sheets can be used.*				
2. All cover sheets must carry a statement of disclaimer to guard the privacy of the patient. A **disclaimer** is a statement of denial of legal liability. A disclaimer should be included on the cover sheet and may read something like the following: *This fax contains confidential or proprietary information that may be legally privileged. It is intended only for the named recipient(s). If an addressing or transmission error has misdirected the fax, please notify the author by replying to this message. If you are not the named recipient, you are not authorized to use, disclose, distribute, copy, print, or rely on this fax and should immediately shred it.**				
3. Place all pages of the document, including the cover sheet, either face down or face up in the fax machine's sending tray, depending on the directions stamped on the sending tray.				
4. If the documents are placed face down, write the area code and fax number on the back of the last page.				

(continued)

Name ____________________ Class ____________ Date ________

Procedure Steps Total Possible Points - 48 Time Limit: 10 minutes	Practice #1	Practice #2	Practice #3	Final
5. Dial the telephone number of the receiving fax machine, using either the telephone attached to the fax machine or the numbers on the fax keyboard. Include the area code for long-distance calls.				
6. When using a fax telephone, listen for a high-pitched tone. Then press the "Send" or "Start" button and hang up the telephone. This step completes the call circuit in older-model fax machines. Your fax is now being sent. Newer fax machines do not require this step.*				
7. If you use the fax keyboard, press the "Send" or "Start" button after dialing the telephone number. This button will start the call.				
8. Watch for the fax machine to make a connection. Often a green light appears as the document feeds through the machine.				
9. If the fax machine is not able to make a connection, as when the receiving fax line is busy, it may have a feature that automatically redials the number every few minutes for a specified number of attempts.				
10. When a fax has been successfully sent, most fax machines print a confirmation message. When a fax has not been sent, the machine either prints an error message or indicates on the screen that the transmission was unsuccessful.*				
11. Attach the confirmation or error message to the documents faxed. File appropriately.*				
12. The sender may call the recipient to confirm that the fax was received.				
Total Number of Points Achieved/Final Score				
Initials of Observer:				

Comments and Signatures

Reviewer's comments and signatures:

1. ______________________________

2. ______________________________

3. ______________________________

Instructor's comments:

____

PROCEDURE 5.2 USING A PHOTOCOPIER MACHINE

Procedure Goal

To produce copies of documents

Name ______________________ Class ______________ Date __________

Scoring System

To score each step, use the following scoring system:
1 = poor, 2 = fair, 3 = good, 4 = excellent

A minimum score of at least a 3 must be achieved on **each** step to achieve successful completion of the technique. Detailed instructions on the scoring system are found on page x of the Preface.

Materials

Copier machine, copy paper, documents to be copied

Procedure

Procedure Steps Total Possible Points - 28 Time Limit: 5 minutes	Practice #1	Practice #2	Practice #3	Final
1. Make sure the machine is turned on and warmed up. It will display a signal when it is ready for copying. 2. Assemble and prepare your materials, removing paper clips, staples, and self-adhesive flags.* 3. Place the document to be copied in the automatic feeder tray as directed, or upside down directly on the glass. The feeder tray can accommodate many pages; you may place only one page at a time on the glass. Automatic feeding is a faster process, and you should use it when you wish to collate or staple packets. Page-by-page copying is best if you need to copy a single sheet or to enlarge or reduce the image. To use any special features, such as making double-sided copies or stapling the copies, press a designated button on the machine. 4. Set the machine for the desired paper size.* 5. Key in the number of copies you want to make, and press the "Start" button. The copies are made automatically. 6. Press the "Clear" or "Reset" button when your job is finished.* 7. If the copier becomes jammed, follow the directions on the machine to locate the problem (for example, there may be multiple pieces of paper stuck inside the printer) and dislodge the jammed paper. Most copy machines will show a diagram of the printer and the location of the problem.				
Total Number of Points Achieved/Final Score				
Initials of Observer:				

Comments and Signatures

Reviewer's comments and signatures:

1. ______________________________

2. ______________________________

3. ______________________________

Instructor's comments:

____

Name ______________________ Class ______________ Date ________

PROCEDURE 5.3 USING A POSTAGE METER

Procedure Goal

To correctly apply postage to an envelope or package for mailing, according to U.S. Postal Service guidelines

Materials

Postage meter, addressed envelope or package, postal scale

Scoring System

To score each step, use the following scoring system:
1 = poor, 2 = fair, 3 = good, 4 = excellent

A minimum score of at least a 3 must be achieved on **each** step to achieve successful completion of the technique. Detailed instructions on the scoring system are found on page x of the Preface.

Procedure

Procedure Steps Total Possible Points - 40 Time Limit: 10 minutes	Practice #1	Practice #2	Practice #3	Final
1. Check that there is postage available in the postage meter.*				
2. Verify the day's date.*				
3. Check that the postage meter is plugged in and switched on before you proceed.				
4. Locate the area where the meter registers the date. Many machines have a lid that can be flipped up, with rows of numbers underneath. Months are represented numerically, with the number "1" indicating the month of January, "2" indicating February, and so on. Check that the date is correct. If it is incorrect, change the numbers to the correct date.				
5. Make sure that all materials have been included in the envelope or package. Weigh the envelope or package on a postal scale. Standard business envelopes weighing up to 1 oz require the minimum postage (the equivalent of one first-class stamp). Oversize envelopes and packages require additional postage. A postal scale will indicate the amount of postage required.				
6. Key in the postage amount on the meter and press the button that enters the amount. For amounts over $1, press the "$" sign or the "Enter" button twice.*				
7. Check that the amount you typed is the correct amount. Envelopes and packages with too little postage will be returned by the U.S. Postal Service. Sending an envelope or package with too much postage is wasteful to the practice.				
8. While applying postage to an envelope, hold it flat and right side up (so that you can read the address). Seal the envelope (unless the meter seals it for you). Locate the plate or area where the envelope slides through. This feature is usually near the bottom of the meter. Place the envelope on the left side, and give it a gentle push toward the right. Some models hold the envelope in a stationary position. (If the meter seals the envelope for you, it is especially important that you insert it correctly to allow for sealing.) The meter will grab the envelope and pull it through quickly.				

(continued)

Name ______________________ Class ______________ Date ____________

Procedure Steps Total Possible Points - 40 Time Limit: 10 minutes	Practice #1	Practice #2	Practice #3	Final
9. For packages, create a postage label to affix to the package. Follow the same procedure for a label as for an envelope. Affix the postmarked label on the package in the upper-right corner. 10. Check that the printed postmark has the correct date and amount and that everything written or stamped on the envelope or package is legible.				
Total Number of Points Achieved/Final Score				
Initials of Observer:				

Comments and Signatures

Reviewer's comments and signatures:

1. ______________________________

2. ______________________________

3. ______________________________

Instructor's comments:

____

Procedure 5.4 Using a Dictation-Transcription Machine

Procedure Goal

To correctly use a dictation-transcription machine to convert verbal communication into the written word

Materials

Dictation-transcription machine, audiocassette or magnetic tape or disk with the recorded dictation, word processor or computer, and printer

Scoring System

To score each step, use the following scoring system:
1 = poor, 2 = fair, 3 = good, 4 = excellent

A minimum score of at least a 3 must be achieved on **each** step to achieve successful completion of the technique. Detailed instructions on the scoring system are found on page x of the Preface.

Name ______________________ Class ______________ Date ____________

Procedure

Procedure Steps Total Possible Points - 40 Time Limit: 20 minutes	Practice #1	Practice #2	Practice #3	Final
1. Assemble all the necessary equipment.				
2. Select a dictation tape, cassette, or disk for transcription. Select any transcriptions marked "Urgent" first. If there are none, select the oldest dated transcription first.*				
3. Turn on all equipment and adjust it according to personal preference.*				
4. Prepare the format and style for the selected letter or form.				
5. Insert the tape or cassette and rewind.*				
6. While listening to the transcription tape, cassette, or disk, key in the text.				
7. Adjust the speed and volume controls as needed.				
8. Proofread and spell check final document, making any corrections.*				
9. Print the document for approval and signature.				
10. Turn off all equipment. Place the transcription tape, cassette, or disk in the proper storage area.				
Total Number of Points Achieved/Final Score				
Initials of Observer:				

Comments and Signatures

Reviewer's comments and signatures:

1. ______________________________

2. ______________________________

3. ______________________________

Instructor's comments:

____

Procedure 5.5 Using a Check-Writing Machine

Procedure Goal

To produce a check using a check-writing machine

Materials

Check-writing machine, blank checks, office checkbook or accounting system

Name ______________________ Class ______________ Date __________

Scoring System

To score each step, use the following scoring system:
1 = poor, 2 = fair, 3 = good, 4 = excellent

A minimum score of at least a 3 must be achieved on **each** step to achieve successful completion of the technique. Detailed instructions on the scoring system are found on page x of the Preface.

Procedure

Procedure Steps Total Possible Points - 40 Time Limit: 10 minutes	**Practice #1**	**Practice #2**	**Practice #3**	**Final**
1. Assemble all equipment.				
2. Turn on the check-writing machine.				
3. Place a blank check or a sheet of blank checks into the machine.				
4. Key in the date, the payee's name, and the payment amount. The check-writing machine imprints the check with this information, perforating it with the payee's name. The perforations are actual little holes in the paper, which prevent anyone from changing the name on the check.				
5. Turn off the check-writing machine.				
6. A doctor or another authorized person then signs the check.*				
7. To complete the process, record the check in the office checkbook or accounting system.*				
Total Number of Points Achieved/Final Score				
Initials of Observer:				

Comments and Signatures

Reviewer's comments and signatures:

1. ____________________

2. ____________________

3. ____________________

Instructor's comments:

____

Name ______________________ Class ______________ Date __________

CHAPTER 6

Using Computers in the Office

REVIEW

Vocabulary Review

Matching

Match the key terms in the right column with the definitions in the left column by placing the letter of each correct answer in the space provided.

_______ **1.** The physical components of a computer system

_______ **2.** A blinking line on the computer screen showing where the next character that is keyed will appear

_______ **3.** A device that is used to input printed matter and convert it into a format that can be read by a computer

_______ **4.** The main circuit board that controls the other components in the computer system

_______ **5.** A computer's temporary, programmable memory

_______ **6.** A computer disk similar to an audio compact disc that stores huge amounts of data

_______ **7.** Software that uses more than one medium—such as graphics, sound, and text—to convey information

_______ **8.** A printout of information from a computer

_______ **9.** A type of machine that forms characters using a series of dots created by tiny drops of ink

_______ **10.** A system that allows users to run two or more software programs simultaneously

_______ **11.** A collection of records created and stored on a computer

_______ **12.** A method of sending and receiving messages through a network

_______ **13.** A global network of computers

_______ **14.** A software package that automatically changes the computer monitor at short intervals or shows moving images to prevent burn-in

a. CD-ROM
b. cursor
c. database
d. electronic mail
e. hard copy
f. hardware
g. ink-jet printer
h. Internet
i. motherboard
j. multimedia
k. multitasking
l. random-access memory (RAM)
m. scanner
n. screen saver

Name ____________________ Class ____________ Date ________

True or False

Decide whether each statement is true or false. In the space at the left, write T *for true or* F *for false. On the lines provided, rewrite the false statements to make them true.*

______ **15.** It is important to back up computer files and store them properly.

____

______ **16.** Telemedicine refers to the use of telecommunications to transmit video images of patient information.

____

______ **17.** CD-R technology enables the computer to comprehend and interpret spoken words.

____

______ **18.** Read-only memory (ROM) can be read by the computer, but you cannot make changes to it.

____

______ **19.** Random-access memory (RAM) provides speed to the computer. The more RAM, the faster the computer will perform.

____

______ **20.** To relieve the symptoms of carpal tunnel syndrome, hands while typing should be lowered below the waist.

____

______ **21.** The software is where information is stored permanently for later retrieval.

____

______ **22.** The central processing unit (CPU) is also called a microprocessor.

____

______ **23.** The blinking line or cube on the computer screen showing where the next character that is keyed will appear is called the pointing device.

____

______ **24.** A scanner is helpful in a medical office because patient reports from another doctor, a hospital, or another outside source can easily be entered into the computer.

____

Content Review

Multiple Choice

In the space provided, write the letter of the choice that best completes each statement or answers each question.

______ **1.** Another name for a laptop is a

A. minicomputer.

B. mainframe.

C. notebook.

D. microcomputer.

_______ **2.** A subnotebook
- **A.** is also called a laptop.
- **B.** is not really a computer because it is too small to function fully.
- **C.** does not require software.
- **D.** is a miniature computer.
- **E.** is better than a palmtop.

_______ **3.** The difference between hardware and software is
- **A.** none—there is no difference.
- **B.** hardware is portable and software is not.
- **C.** hardware means the physical parts of a computer system and software is the instructions within the computer system.
- **D.** software is portable and hardware is not.

_______ **4.** The device that made today's computer possible is
- **A.** the abacus.
- **B.** the punch card.
- **C.** the vacuum tube.
- **D.** the micro chip.
- **E.** All of the above.

_______ **5.** The keyboard is the most common input device. Other input devices include
- **A.** a mouse.
- **B.** earphones.
- **C.** software.
- **D.** speakers.
- **E.** file folders.

_______ **6.** Which statement about ROM is *true*?
- **A.** It is permanent memory.
- **B.** It is the same as RAM.
- **C.** It is programmable.
- **D.** You can make changes to ROM.

_______ **7.** The most common type of pointing device is a
- **A.** mouse.
- **B.** scanner.
- **C.** touch pad.
- **D.** keyboard.

_______ **8.** A jump drive is
- **A.** a type of software.
- **B.** a way to provide portability to a large body of information.
- **C.** an internally attached drive.
- **D.** large and heavy.

_______ **9.** A "multitasking" system means
- **A.** many different types of expenses are involved.
- **B.** the system has multiple uses.
- **C.** users can run two or more software programs simultaneously.
- **D.** None of the above.

_______ **10.** The term *software* means
  A. portable hardware.
  B. physical computer components.
  C. the input device.
  D. a set of instructions or program that tells the computer what to do.

_______ **11.** Which of the following is considered the most important piece of hardware in a computer system?
  A. RAM
  B. ROM
  C. The USB port
  D. The instruction set
  E. The CPU

_______ **12.** A zip drive is
  A. faster software.
  B. a high-capacity floppy disc drive.
  C. a type of mouse.
  D. the same as a jump drive.

_______ **13.** *Resolution* refers to
  A. color.
  B. the size of an image.
  C. the sound and clarity of a speaker system.
  D. the crispness of the images and is measured in dot pitch.

_______ **14.** Which of the following statements about DOS is *true*?
  A. It is dependant on the use of function keys.
  B. It represents the most up-to-date technology.
  C. It is easier to use than a Windows system.
  D. None of these statements is true.

_______ **15.** A database is
  A. a document.
  B. a collection of records created and stored on a computer.
  C. the software used by a computer.
  D. the hardware of a computer.

_______ **16.** E-mail etiquette is
  A. established when a practice creates a written e-mail policy spelling out the "dos" and "don'ts" concerning the use of the company's e-mail system.
  B. determined by each individual employee.
  C. not essential in a place of business.
  D. None of the above.

_______ **17.** A search engine is
  A. part of the computer.
  B. part of the software for a computer.
  C. a specialized website that connects with other websites for information.
  D. purchased annually.

Name ________________________________ Class ____________________ Date ____________

_______ **18.** The first step in selecting new computer equipment is

- **A.** to set up a trial run of a new system for 30 days.
- **B.** to research into the needs of the office and the capabilities of the equipment.
- **C.** to remove the old system.
- **D.** to convert back to a manual system.

_______ **19.** A CD-R

- **A.** is another name for a CD-ROM.
- **B.** is the same as a CD.
- **C.** allows for information to be taken from a source and stored to a CD.
- **D.** is a type of modem.

_______ **20.** A computer password

- **A.** backs up computer files.
- **B.** can be shared by more than one employee performing the same functions.
- **C.** stores information.
- **D.** helps protect computer files.

Sentence Completion

In the space provided, write the word or phrase that best completes each sentence.

21. A _______ is a modem that operates over cable television lines to provide fast Internet access.

22. _______ is a measurement of how many instructions per second that the CPU can process.

23. Carpal tunnel syndrome is caused by _______ hand and finger motions.

24. The speed at which a computer can process information depends on the type and speed of its _______.

25. A _______ modem operates over telephone lines but uses a different frequency than the telephone frequency.

26. Word processing, database, and accounting software are examples of software that is written for a specific purpose, or _______.

27. _______ are high-resolution printers that use a technology similar to that of photocopiers.

28. Requiring a(n) _______ limits the computer users who can access files.

29. A _______ is a device used to input printed matter and convert it into a format that the computer can read.

30. _______ is a measurement of how much information can be sent or processed with one single instruction, and is calculated in bits or bytes.

31. A _______ is a computer that is very small and light. It cannot perform all the functions of a notebook computer but can be useful for people who need to have a computer available while they are out of the office.

32. To use a modem, you must have access to a _______.

21. ______________________________

22. ______________________________

23. ______________________________

24. ______________________________

25. ______________________________

26. ______________________________

27. ______________________________

28. ______________________________

29. ______________________________

30. ______________________________

31. ______________________________

32. ______________________________

33. Photocopiers can be configured with a _______ and can transmit the images of scanned documents to computers.

34. Users who access computer files can be identified with _______.

35. A _______ is a type of pointing device and is common on laptop and notebook computers.

33. ______________________

34. ______________________

35. ______________________

Short Answer

Write the answer to each question on the lines provided.

36. Compare a mouse and a trackball.

____

____

____

37. Give one advantage and one disadvantage of a fax modem.

____

____

____

38. Compare a diskette and a CD-ROM.

____

____

____

39. What is the advantage of a dot matrix printer over a laser printer?

____

____

____

40. What are two advantages of a Windows operating system over a DOS system?

____

____

____

41. Patient records are stored on the hard disk drive of a computer. What are three ways that you could give a copy of those records to a consulting physician?

____

____

____

42. What are four kinds of medical information that you could find using the Internet?

____

____

____

43. What are three sources of information you might turn to if you are having problems using a software program?

____

____

____

44. How does a surge protector help maintain a computer system?

____

____

____

45. What should you do to protect diskettes from damage?

____

____

____

46. Based on what you have learned, write a list of general guidelines for purchasing a computer system for a medical practice.

____

____

____

47. Describe the purpose of OCR software.

____

____

____

48. Define and describe a virtual private network.

____

____

____

Critical Thinking

Write the answer to each question on the lines provided.

1. If a medical office can afford only one computer, what kind should it purchase? Explain your answer.

____

____

____

2. Why might it be useful to add a fax modem to a computer system even though the medical office already has a regular fax machine?

____

____

____

3. Why might it be a good idea to take a computer course at an adult school or community college every few years?

____

____

____

4. When buying a computer system, why is it a good idea to purchase all components from one vendor?

____

____

____

5. How might a large medical office benefit from adding CD-R technology to its computer system?

____

____

____

6. Why is it a good idea to use a screen saver designed to come on after only one minute of inactivity on a computer near a patient reception area?

____

____

____

7. Describe a computer disaster recovery plan.

____

____

____

APPLICATION

Follow the directions for the application.

Typing and Editing a Letter on the Computer

a. Open a new file on your word processing program and type the letter below.

November 4, 2008

Mr. Karl Cousin 24 Elm St.
Wilmington, NJ 12345

Dear Mr. Cousin:

I have been unable to reach you by phone, so I am writing to confirm your appointment for Wednesday, November 9, at 2:30 PM. If you will be unable to keep this appointment, please call us immediately at 555-7890 to cancel it or to change your appointment time. If we do not hear from you by Tuesday, November 8, at 2:30 PM, we will assume you will keep the appointment, and you will be charged for the visit.

Please remember that payment must be made at the time of your appointment unless you have made other arrangements with our office. Be sure to bring any pertinent insurance forms with you and give them to us. We appreciate your cooperation and look forward to seeing you at our office on November 9.

Sincerely,

Marty Miller
Office Manager

b. Print a hard copy of your letter. Then make these changes to the computer file:

  1. In the inside address, add the patient's middle name: *James.*

  2. Spell out the word *Street.*

  3. In the second paragraph, delete these words: *and give them to us.*

  4. Move the last sentence of the letter to the beginning of the second paragraph.

  5. Save the letter under this file name: *confirm.apt.*

  6. Print a hard copy of your revision of the letter.

c. Now open a new file and write another letter that a medical office might send to a patient, a newly hired staff person, or a laboratory, hospital, or consulting physician.

  1. Print a hard copy of your first draft.

  2. Exchange letters with a partner and suggest any changes that would improve his letter.

  3. Use the computer function keys to improve your letter by adding, deleting, and moving information.

  4. Print your final version.

Case Studies

Write your response to each case study on the lines provided.

Case 1

The medical office where you work has just begun converting to a computer system. The doctors are concerned about the confidentiality of the files. What will you recommend?

____

____

____

Case 2

A coworker is intimidated by the office's new word processing program. Nearly every day she hands you a letter she has handwritten and begs you to enter it on the computer and print it so she can send it out. You are getting behind in your own work as a result. How can you solve this problem and still maintain a positive relationship with your coworker?

____

____

____

Case 3

You enjoy painting with watercolors, but lately you have had trouble opening the paint containers and controlling the brush. A few months ago your office converted to a computerized record-keeping system. Explain a possible connection and how you would address this problem.

____

____

____

Name ______________________ Class ______________ Date __________

Procedure Competency Checklist

Procedure 6.1 Creating a Form Letter

Procedure Goal

To use a word processing program to create a form letter

Scoring System

To score each step, use the following scoring system:
1 = poor, 2 = fair, 3 = good, 4 = excellent

A minimum score of at least a 3 must be achieved on **each** step to achieve successful completion of the technique. Detailed instructions on the scoring system are found on page x of the Preface.

Materials

Computer equipped with a word processing program, printer, form letter to be created, 8½- by 11-inch paper.

Procedure

Procedure Steps Total Possible Points - 32 Time Limit: 10 minutes	Practice #1	Practice #2	Practice #3	Final
1. Turn on the computer. Select the word processing program.				
2. Use the keyboard to begin entering text into a new document.				
3. To edit text, press the arrow keys to move the cursor to the position at which you want to insert or delete characters, and enter the text. Either type directly or use the "Insert" mode to type over and replace existing text.				
4. To delete text, position the cursor to the left of the characters to be deleted and press the "Delete" key. Alternatively, place the cursor to the right of the characters to be deleted and press the "Backspace" key (the left-pointing arrow usually found at the top-right corner of the keyboard).				
5. If you need to move an entire block of text, you must begin by highlighting it. In most Windows-based programs, you first click the mouse at the beginning of the text to be highlighted. Then you hold down the left mouse button, drag the mouse to the end of the block of text, and release your finger from the mouse. The text should now be highlighted. Choose the button or command for cutting text. Then move the cursor to the place where you want to insert the text and select the button or command for retrieving or pasting text.				
6. As you input the letter, it is important to save your work every 15 minutes or so. Some programs do this automatically. If yours does not, use the "Save" command or button to save the file. Be sure to save the file again when you have completed the letter.*				

(continued)

Name ______________________ Class ______________ Date ____________

Procedure Steps Total Possible Points - 32 Time Limit: 10 minutes	Practice #1	Practice #2	Practice #3	Final
7. Carefully proofread the document and use the spell checker, correcting any errors in spelling or formatting.* 8. Print the letter using the "Print" command or button.				
Total Number of Points Achieved/Final Score				
Initials of Observer:				

Comments and Signatures

Reviewer's comments and signatures:

1. ______________________________

2. ______________________________

3. ______________________________

Instructor's comments:

____

Name ______________________ Class ______________ Date ______________

CHAPTER 7

Managing Correspondence and Mail

Review

Vocabulary Review

Passage Completion

Study the key terms in the box. Use your textbook to find definitions of terms you do not understand.

annotate	courtesy title	letterhead
body	dateline	modified-block letter style
clarity	editing	proofreading
complimentary closing	full-block letter style	salutation
concise	identification line	simplified letter style

In the space provided, complete the following passage, using some of the terms from the box. You may change the form of a term to fit the meaning of the sentence.

Most business letters are written on (1) _______ paper, which identifies the business. The (2) _______, which is placed about three lines below the preprinted letterhead text, gives the day, month, and year. In the inside address, the receiver's name usually includes a(n)(3) _______, such as Dr. or Mrs. The receiver's name is repeated in the (4) _______. In the (5) _______, or block style, all lines are flush left. In the (6) _______, the dateline, complimentary closing, and other parts of the letter begin at about the center of the page. The (7) _______ omits the salutation and the complimentary closing.

1. ______________________

2. ______________________

3. ______________________

4. ______________________

5. ______________________

6. ______________________

7. ______________________

True or False

Decide whether each statement is true or false. In the space at the left, write T *for true or* F *for false. On the lines provided, rewrite the false statements to make them true.*

_______ **8.** Tan kraft envelopes are also called clasp envelopes.

____

Name ______________________ Class ______________ Date __________

_______ 9. The standard setting for margin in business correspondence is 2 inches.

____

_______ 10. You need to capitalize all the words in the closing of a business letter.

____

_______ 11. The USPS abbreviation PA stands for *Pennsylvania.*

____

Content Review

Sentence Completion

In the space provided, write the word or phrase that best completes each sentence.

1. The _______ is similar to full block but it differs in that the dateline, complimentary closing, signature block, and notations are aligned and begin at the center of the page or slightly to the right.
2. Two different styles of punctuation used in correspondence are _______ and _______.
3. The USPS abbreviation for Kansas is _______.
4. _______ include information such as the number of enclosures that are included with the letter and the names of other people who will be receiving copies of the letter.
5. _______ means thoroughly checking a document for errors.
6. The USPS uses electronic _______ to help speed mail processing.
7. The web address for the U.S. Postal Service web page is _______.
8. The USPS abbreviation for *center* is _______.
9. Most correspondence generated in a medical office, such as letters, postcards, and invoices, is sent by _______.
10. _______ is also called parcel post.
11. The first step in processing mail is _______ it.
12. To _______ means to underline or highlight key points of the letter or to write reminders, comments, or suggested actions in the margins or on self-adhesive notes.
13. Business letters written with the modified-block letter style with indented paragraphs are identical to the modified-block style except that the paragraphs are _______.
14. When writing a business letter, it is proper to include at least _______ in each paragraph.
15. "Enc" in a business letter means _______.

1. ______________________
2. ______________________
3. ______________________
4. ______________________
5. ______________________
6. ______________________
7. ______________________
8. ______________________
9. ______________________
10. ______________________
11. ______________________
12. ______________________
13. ______________________
14. ______________________
15. ______________________

16. The space around the edges of a form or letter that is left blank is called the _______.

17. The _______ of a letter consists of single-spaced lines that are the content of a business letter.

18. _______, which can be printed from a computerized mailing list, can greatly speed the process of addressing envelopes for bulk mailings.

19. The most common envelope size used for correspondence is the _______.

20. _______ is the action the post office will take when a piece of mail does not reach its destination.

21. _______ written on the outside of a letter or package means that the letter or package should not be opened by anyone but the addressee.

22. _______ is the process that ensures that a document is accurate, clear, and complete; free of grammatical errors; organized logically; and written in an appropriate style.

16. ____________________

17. ____________________

18. ____________________

19. ____________________

20. ____________________

21. ____________________

22. ____________________

Short Answer

Write the answer to each question on the lines provided.

23. What are some advantages of learning to manage correspondence for a medical office in a professional manner?

____

____

____

24. List three types of envelopes commonly used in a medical office, and briefly describe their uses.

____

____

____

25. What is the difference between a modified-block letter style and a simplified letter style?

____

____

____

26. Describe the voice of the sentence below. Then rewrite the sentence, changing the voice to make it more direct and concise.

    The patient's blood sample was sent to you by our office on November 4, 2007.

____

____

____

27. How do editing and proofreading differ?

28. Why is an envelope with a typed address likely to be delivered more quickly than one with a handwritten address?

29. Describe an accordion fold on a business letter, and explain why it is used.

30. Describe a situation in which an item might be sent by fourth-class mail from a medical office.

31. When processing incoming mail, why is it important to check the address on each letter or package?

32. Describe the difference between certified and registered mail.

Critical Thinking

Write the answer to each question on the lines provided.

1. As an assistant in a new medical practice, what correspondence supply would you order first? Explain your answer.

2. Briefly describe two types of letters from a health-care professional in which the tone should be formal and two types in which the tone could be relaxed.

3. Which of these errors could be considered most serious: a formatting error, a data error, or a mechanical error? Explain your answer.

4. Why should a medical assistant take the time to learn and use the rules of spelling, punctuation, and capitalization?

5. What are three problems that could occur if a medical assistant handled incoming mail in a disorganized way?

Application

Follow the directions for each application.

1. **Applying Basic Rules of Effective Writing**

   Read each of the following sentences for errors in spelling, word division, and capitalization and in the use of plurals, possessives, and numbers. If a sentence is incorrect, rewrite it correctly on the lines provided. Compare your corrections with those of a partner. Did you find the same errors? Did you miss any? Are there any writing rules that you need to study further?

   a. The Patients left oricle showed evidence of a recent infarktion.

   b. The abcess developed during the patients' recent trip to see his aunt.

   c. The patient was given a perscription for a 10-day supply of ilosone, a form of erythromycin.

   d. This 6-year-old patient reports falling from a slide at Ridge Street school this past tuesday.

e. X-rays indicate hare-line fraktures of two cervical vertebra.

f. Vigorous work outdoors in hot tempratures apparantly aggravated pastor Henrys heart condition.

2. Handling Incoming Mail

Assume that you are a medical assistant whose duties include processing incoming mail. Some of the procedures that you follow are described below. For procedures that are correct, write *correct* on the lines provided. For procedures that are incorrect, write the correct procedures on the lines provided.

a. Collect everything from the office mailbox and process it a few items at a time throughout the day.

b. In the top-priority pile, place letters and packages sent by overnight mail delivery, special delivery, registered mail, or certified mail. To this pile, also add any newspapers or magazines.

c. After sorting the mail, open all the envelopes at once—except for those marked "personal" or "confidential"—and remove their contents, making sure to take everything out of each envelope.

d. Throw away the envelopes as soon as you have removed their contents.

e. Compare enclosure notations on each letter with the actual enclosures to make sure all items were included. Then make notes about missing items so that senders can be contacted.

f. Staple each letter to its enclosures so they cannot become separated.

g. Stamp any bills or statements with the date they are received.

3. Preparing a Business Letter

Read the following case study: You are a medical assistant working in a busy family practice office. One of the physicians says to you, "Please prepare a letter to go to Mr. Ford. He is the attorney for Mrs. Smith. Just check her chart to get his address. Tell him that Mrs. Smith has not been coming to her scheduled appointments. Tell him that I can't help her if she doesn't want my help!"

What questions might you have before you prepare this letter?

4. Commonly Misspelled Words

Correct the spelling of the following words.

a. __________ abcess

b. __________ laynx

c. __________ chancrer

d. __________ nocomial

e. __________ defibillator

f. __________ parentral

g. __________ sphymomanometer

h. __________ Febuary

i. __________ comittee

j. __________ occassion

k. __________ truely

CASE STUDIES

Write your response to each case study on the lines provided.

Case 1

A new coworker asks you to proofread a business letter that he wrote. You notice that the letter contains numerous formatting and mechanical errors. You also suspect that there may be data errors in the letter. What should you do?

Case 2

You have just finished preparing several letters for signing by Dr. Morris, a physician in your office. Most of the letters need to be sent out today, but he will be extremely busy with patients for the rest of the day. Dr. Fuchs, another physician in your office, has authorized you to sign her letters. Should you sign Dr. Morris's letters and send them out right away? Explain your answer.

____

____

____

Case 3

While opening the office mail, you discover that a patient has enclosed a check for more than she owes. Should you take a moment from processing the mail to call the patient? Why or why not?

____

____

____

Case 4

A patient has come to your office without an appointment because he has unexpectedly run out of a prescription heart medication. The physician's schedule is completely full, so you cannot give the patient an appointment. However, you know that samples of this drug are in the sample cabinet. The patient should not skip any doses of this medication. What should you do?

____

____

____

Procedure Competency Checklists

Procedure 7.1 Creating a Letter

Procedure Goal

To follow standard procedure for constructing a business letter

Scoring System

To score each step, use the following scoring system:
1 = poor, 2 = fair, 3 = good, 4 = excellent

A minimum score of at least a 3 must be achieved on **each** step to achieve successful completion of the technique. Detailed instructions on the scoring system are found on page x of the Preface.

Materials

Word processor or personal computer, letterhead paper, dictionaries or other sources

Name ______________________ Class ______________ Date __________

Procedure

Procedure Steps Total Possible Points - 60 Time Limit: 15 minutes	Practice #1	Practice #2	Practice #3	Final
1. Format the letter according to the office's standard procedure. Use the same punctuation and style throughout.*				
2. Start the dateline three lines below the last line of the printed letterhead. (Note: Depending on the length of the letter, it is acceptable to start between two and six lines below the letterhead.)*				
3. Two lines below the dateline, type in any special mailing instructions (such as REGISTERED MAIL, CERTIFIED MAIL, and so on).				
4. Three lines below any special instructions, begin the inside address. Type the addressee's courtesy title (Mr., Mrs., Ms.) and full name on the first line. If a professional title is given (M.D., RN, Ph.D.), type this title after the addressee's name instead of using a courtesy title.*				
5. Type the addressee's business title, if applicable, on the second line. Type the company name on the third line. Type the street address on the fourth line, including the apartment or suite number. Type the city, state, and zip code on the fifth line. Use the standard two-letter abbreviation for the state, followed by one space and the zip code.*				
6. Two lines below the inside address, type the salutation, using the appropriate courtesy title (Mr., Mrs., Ms., Dr.) prior to typing the addressee's last name.*				
7. Two lines below the salutation, type the subject line, if applicable.				
8. Two lines below the subject line, begin the body of the letter. Single-space between lines. Double-space between paragraphs.				
9. Two lines below the body of the letter, type the complimentary closing.				
10. Leave three blank lines (return four times) and begin the signature block. (Enough space must be left to allow for the signature.) Type the sender's name on the first line. Type the sender's title on the second line.*				
11. Two lines below the sender's title, type the identification line. Type the sender's initials in all capitals and your initials in lowercase letters, separating the two sets of initials with a colon or a forward slash.				
12. One or two lines below the identification line, type the enclosure notation, if applicable.				
13. Two lines below the enclosure notation, type the copy notation, if applicable.				

(continued)

Name ______________________ Class ______________ Date ____________

Procedure Steps Total Possible Points - 60 Time Limit: 15 minutes	Practice #1	Practice #2	Practice #3	Final
14. Edit the letter.* 15. Proofread and spell check the letter.*				
Total Number of Points Achieved/Final Score				
Initials of Observer:				

Comments and Signatures

Reviewer's comments and signatures:

1. ______________________________

2. ______________________________

3. ______________________________

Instructor's comments:

____

Procedure 7.2 Sorting and Opening Mail

Procedure Goal

To follow a standard procedure for sorting, opening, and processing incoming office mail

Scoring System

To score each step, use the following scoring system:
1 = poor, 2 = fair, 3 = good, 4 = excellent

A minimum score of at least a 3 must be achieved on **each** step to achieve successful completion of the technique. Detailed instructions on the scoring system are found on page x of the Preface.

Materials

Letter opener, date and time stamp (manual or automatic), stapler, paper clips, adhesive notes

Procedure

Procedure Steps Total Possible Points - 56 Time Limit: 10 minutes	Practice #1	Practice #2	Practice #3	Final
1. Check the address on each letter or package to be sure that it has been delivered to the correct location. 2. Sort the mail into piles according to priority and type of mail. Your system may include the following: • Top priority. This pile will contain any items that were sent by overnight mail delivery in addition to items sent by registered mail, certified mail, or special delivery. (Faxes and e-mail messages are also top priority.) • Second priority. This pile will include personal or confidential mail.				

(continued)

Name ______________________ Class ______________ Date ____________

Procedure Steps Total Possible Points - 56 Time Limit: 10 minutes	Practice #1	Practice #2	Practice #3	Final
• Third priority. This pile will contain all first-class mail, airmail, and Priority Mail items. These items should be divided into payments received, insurance forms, reports, and other correspondence. • Fourth priority. This pile will consist of packages. • Fifth priority. This pile will contain magazines and newspapers. • Sixth priority. This last pile will include advertisements and catalogs.				
3. Set aside all letters labeled "Personal" or "Confidential." Unless you have permission to open these letters, only the addressee should open them.				
4. Arrange all the envelopes with the flaps facing up and away from you.				
5. Tap the lower edge of the envelope to shift the contents to the bottom. This step helps to prevent cutting any of the contents when you open the envelope.				
6. Open all the envelopes.*				
7. Remove and unfold the contents, making sure that nothing remains in the envelope.				
8. Review each document and check the sender's name and address. • If the letter has no return address, save the envelope, or cut the address off the envelope and tape it to the letter. • Check to see if the address matches the one on the envelope. If there is a difference, staple the envelope to the letter, and make a note to verify the correct address with the sender.				
9. Compare the enclosure notation on the letter with the actual enclosures to make sure that all items are included. Make a note to contact the sender if anything is missing.				
10. Clip together each letter and its enclosures.				
11. Check the date of the letter. If there is a significant delay between the date of the letter and the postmark, keep the envelope.*				
12. If all contents appear to be in order, you can discard the envelope.				
13. Review all bills and statements. • Make sure the amount enclosed is the same as the amount listed on the statement. • Make a note of any discrepancies.				

(continued)

Name ______________________ Class ______________ Date __________

Procedure Steps Total Possible Points - 56 Time Limit: 10 minutes	Practice #1	Practice #2	Practice #3	Final
14. Stamp each piece of correspondence with the date (and sometimes the time) to record its receipt. If possible, stamp each item in the same location—such as the upper-right corner.*				
Total Number of Points Achieved/Final Score				
Initials of Observer:				

Comments and Signatures

Reviewer's comments and signatures:

1. ____

2. ____

3. ____

Instructor's comments:

____

Name ______________________ Class ______________ Date __________

CHAPTER 8

Managing Office Supplies

REVIEW

Vocabulary Review

True or False

Decide whether each statement is true or false. In the space at the left, write T *for true or* F *for false. On the lines provided, rewrite the false statements to make them true.*

_______ **1.** A medical assistant should avoid storing boxes or supplies near a water heater, air-conditioning unit, heater, or stove.

____

_______ **2.** Paper cups are considered an administrative supply expense.

____

_______ **3.** The list of supplies the office uses regularly and the quantity in storage constitute the office inventory.

____

_______ **4.** The average medical practice spends between 10% and 15% of its annual gross income on administrative, clinical, and general supplies.

____

_______ **5.** A durable item is an item that is used indefinitely.

____

_______ **6.** When you receive a shipment or an order, it is important to check the invoice carefully against the original order and the packing slip.

____

_______ **7.** If an invoice says "Net 30," you have 30 days in which to pay the total amount of the invoice without penalty charges.

____

_______ **8.** When ordering by fax, it is always best to use the form provided by the vendor.

____

_______ **9.** A purchase order does not require an authorizing signature.

____

_______ **10.** A disbursement is a payment of funds.

____

Name ______________________ Class ______________ Date ____________

_______ **11.** Purchasing groups get the same prices as an individual ordering because the law requires equal pricing.

____

_______ **12.** The unit price of an item is the price per item.

____

_______ **13.** With most vendors, "rush orders" cost the same as orders delivered by standard shipping.

____

_______ **14.** It is a good idea to take advantage of phone solicitations to help control costs of supplies.

____

_______ **15.** The word "supplies" refers to expendable items or items that are used up and restocked.

____

Passage Completion

Study the key terms in the box. Use your textbook to find definitions of terms you do not understand.

unit price	vital	disbursement
rush order	invoice	reorder reminder cards
clinical	Material Safety Data Sheet (MSDS)	inventory card or record page
administrative	computerized inventory system	

In the space provided, complete the following passage, using some of the terms from the box. You may change the form of a term to fit the meaning of the sentence.

In a medical office, a(n) (16) _______ for each item or category of items may be a 4 × 6 inch index card or a page in a loose-leaf binder. (17) _______ are usually brightly colored cards inserted directly into stock on the supply shelf to indicate when it is time to reorder. A(n) (18) _______ is the best choice for a large medical practice. To calculate an item's (19) _______, divide the total price of the package by the quantity, or the number of items. (20) _______ usually cost more than regularly scheduled orders and should be avoided when possible. The information supplied by the manufacturer describing the chemical breakdown of a product is called a(n) (21) _______. A payment of funds to a vendor is called a(n) (22) _______. Another name for a bill is a(n) (23) _______. Alcohol swabs are an example of a(n) (24) _______ supply. Insurance materials are an example of (25) _______ supplies. (26)_______ is a category of supplies that are essential to ensure the smooth running of the practice.

16. ______________________

17. ______________________

18. ______________________

19. ______________________

20. ______________________

21. ______________________

22. ______________________

23. ______________________

24. ______________________

25. ______________________

26. ______________________

Name ______________________ Class ______________ Date ________

Content Review

Multiple Choice

In the space provided, write the letter of the choice that best completes each statement or answers each question.

_____ 1. The best place to store the office's Christmas tree is
- A. in a storage area away from heat and water.
- B. as close to the ceiling as possible because this item is used only once a year.
- C. by the furnace.
- D. near the water heater.
- E. in the patient bathroom.

_____ 2. Which group of items is considered general supplies?
- A. Lancets, tongue depressors, and sutures
- B. Lubricating jelly, alcohol swabs, and needles
- C. Paper cups, toilet paper, and liquid soap
- D. Copy paper, stamps, and pens
- E. File folders, insurance manuals, and forms

_____ 3. Paper administrative supplies should be stored
- A. in an upright position in the original shipping box to save space.
- B. lying flat in the original shipping box.
- C. lying flat after being taken out of the original shipping box.
- D. in an upright position after being taken out of the original shipping box.
- E. in a desk drawer only, after being removed from the original shipping box.

_____ 4. Unit prices are usually lower at larger quantities. Therefore, it makes sense to
- A. buy more items than you need and can store.
- B. buy items in bulk when the purchase can be stored and used within a reasonable amount of time.
- C. never buy items except in large quantities.
- D. not worry about comparative pricing because a small difference in price really doesn't matter.

_____ 5. You should order by "rush order"
- A. only as absolutely required.
- B. on Fridays to avoid the weekend.
- C. routinely.
- D. on Mondays to compensate for the weekend.

_____ 6. The Federal Trade Commission (FTC) requires supply companies to provide merchandise within how many days or to give you the option of canceling with a full refund?
- A. 90
- B. 60
- C. 180
- D. 30

_____ 7. A purchase requisition is
- A. a form that can only be used when faxing an order.
- B. another name for an invoice.
- C. another name for an MSDS sheet.
- D. only used when purchasing through a buying pool.
- E. a formal request from a staff member or doctor.

______ **8.** Most durable items
- **A.** have a short shelf life.
- **B.** must be restocked often.
- **C.** are pieces of equipment that are used indefinitely.
- **D.** are made of paper for easy disposal.

______ **9.** Holiday cards are an example of
- **A.** administrative supplies.
- **B.** general supplies.
- **C.** periodic supplies.
- **D.** noninventoried supplies.

______ **10.** Which items must be stored separately from other products?
- **A.** Liquid soaps
- **B.** Poisons and acids
- **C.** Durable items
- **D.** Bulky items that require a lot of space

Sentence Completion

In the space provided, write the word or phrase that best completes each sentence.

11. Ordering online requires the use of ______ and ______. **11.** ______

12. OSHA stands for ______. **12.** ______

13. The oldest products should be stored on the ______ of the shelf. **13.** ______

14. New calendars and appointment books are examples of ______ supplies. **14.** ______

15. ______ must be stored out of site and in a locked cabinet. **15.** ______

16. If you make a cash disbursement, you should always obtain a ______. **16.** ______

17. The best way to deal with telephone solicitation is ______. **17.** ______

18. Another name for an invoice is a(n) ______. **18.** ______

19. The rules of good housekeeping and ______ apply to storage areas for clinical supplies. **19.** ______

20. ______ are groups of physicians who order supplies together to obtain a quantity discount. **20.** ______

Short Answer

Write the answer to each question on the lines provided.

21. Describe how to establish an online account for ordering supplies.

______

______

______

Name ______________________ Class ______________ Date ____________

22. What tasks are likely to be included in the medical assistant's responsibilities for maintaining supplies?

23. List items that are important to include on an inventory card.

24. Explain how inventory cards and colored adhesive flags can be used to track supplies that must be reordered.

25. Explain the function of reorder reminder cards.

26. Explain how to calculate a unit price.

27. Briefly describe four categories of information you should obtain when investigating a vendor.

28. What procedure should you follow when receiving a supply shipment?

29. Who is inconvenienced when the supply of an important item runs out?

30. Why is it wiser to order in bulk? Give an example.

Name ______________________ Class ______________ Date ________

31. You notice that some items are always running out. What might you do to handle this situation?

32. When preparing a check for a vendor, what information should be included on the front of the check?

33. Why is it important to check an order carefully when it arrives?

Critical Thinking

Write the answer to each question on the lines provided.

1. You have been put in charge of managing supplies for a large practice. You find that this responsibility takes most of your time. You would prefer to have more diverse duties. What might you do?

2. The practice at which you work has been growing quickly. You think you may need to increase the quantity of certain items in the inventory, but you are not sure what quantity would be correct. What should you do?

3. You have heard that ordering medical office supplies through a purchasing group may be less expensive than direct ordering from one office. How might you investigate purchasing groups in your area?

4. A new vendor offers you prices that are far below what you are now paying. You can save the office a great deal of money, but the brands are unknown to you. How should you handle the situation?

Name ______________________ Class ______________ Date __________

5. As you check a shipment of supplies, you discover that there is a greater quantity of one item than was ordered and that one ordered item is missing altogether. What should you do?

____

____

____

APPLICATION

Follow the directions for each application.

1. Inventory Card or Page

You are setting up an inventory system for the office. Your first task is to design inventory pages to place in a binder. What information should you include for each item? List each category of needed information on the lines provided. Use a sheet of paper to design the inventory page.

____

____

____

2. Unit Pricing

You are ordering 2-liter plastic bottles of saline solution for the office. Apex Medical Supply sells a ten-bottle package for $12.50. Acme Medical Supply sells the same brand and size in an eight-bottle package for $11.20. Which package is the better buy?

____

____

____

CASE STUDIES

Write your response to each case study on the lines provided.

Case 1

As the person at your office in charge of ordering supplies, you take a call from an unknown vendor. He tells you that he has an overstock of your brand of photocopier toner. He wants to get rid of it, so he will let you have it for half the regular price. He instructs you to send a check to a box number he gives you; then he will ship the toner to you. What should you do? Why?

____

____

____

Case 2

You have delegated the ordering of all supplies to another employee. Since this assignment, you have noticed that the cost of supplies has steadily increased. What factors could be causing this? What can you do to control the costs?

____

____

____

Case 3

You receive a letter from a vendor threatening collection if an invoice that is now 6 months old is not paid immediately. You know that the invoice has been paid. How can you support your claim that your office has paid its bill?

____

____

____

Case 4

As the new medical assistant at an office, you have been assigned the job of managing supplies. You review the supply-ordering system already in place. You research local supply vendors. Then you decide that the office would benefit by changing vendors for some of its clinical supplies. The doctor has been doing business with the present vendor for years and seems unwilling to change. Still, you ask for time to make a presentation to her and other members of the senior staff. What information should you present to make your case?

____

____

____

Procedure Competency Checklist

Procedure 8.1 Step-by-Step Overview of Inventory Procedures

Procedure Goal

To set up an effective inventory program for a medical office

Scoring System

To score each step, use the following scoring system:
1 = poor, 2 = fair, 3 = good, 4 = excellent

A minimum score of at least a 3 must be achieved on **each** step to achieve successful completion of the technique. Detailed instructions on the scoring system are found on page x of the Preface.

Materials

Pen, paper, file folders, vendor catalogs, index cards or loose-leaf binder and blank pages, reorder reminder cards, vendor order forms

Name ______________________ Class ______________ Date ____________

Procedure

Procedure Steps Total Possible Points - 60 Time Limit: 15 minutes	Practice #1	Practice #2	Practice #3	Final
1. Define with your physician/employer the extent of your responsibility in managing supplies. Know whether the physician's approval or supervision is required for certain procedures, whether any systems have already been established, and if the physician has any preference for a particular vendor or trade-name item. If your medical practice is large, determine which medical assistant is responsible for each aspect of supply management.				
2. Know what administrative and clinical supplies should be stocked in your office. Create a formal supply list of vital, incidental, and periodic items and keep a copy in the office's procedures manual.				
3. Start a file containing a list of current vendors with copies of their catalogs.				
4. Create a wish list of brands or products the office does not currently use but might like to try. Inform other staff members of the list so that they can make entries.				
5. Make a file for supply invoices and completed order forms. (Keep these documents on file for at least 3 years.)*				
6. Devise an inventory system of index cards, loose-leaf pages, or a computer spreadsheet for each item. List the following data for each item on its card: • Date and quantity of each order • Name and contact information for the vendor and sales representative • Date each shipment was received • Total cost and unit cost, or price per piece for the item • Payment method used • Results of periodic counts of the item • Quantity expected to cover the office for a given period of time • Reorder quantity (the quantity remaining on the shelf that indicates when reorder should be made)				
7. Have a system for flagging items that need to be ordered and those that are already on order. For example, mark their cards or pages with a self-adhesive tab or note. Make or buy reorder reminder cards to put into the stock of each item at the reorder quantity level.*				
8. Establish with the physician a regular schedule for taking inventory. Every 1 to 2 weeks is usually sufficient. As a backup system for remembering to check stock and reorder, estimate the times for these activities. Mark them on your calendar or create a tickler file on your computer.*				
9. Order at the same times each week or month, after inventory is taken. However, if there is an unexpected shortage of an item, and more than a week or so remains before the regular ordering time, place the order immediately.				

(continued)

Name ______________________ Class ______________ Date __________

Procedure Steps Total Possible Points - 60 Time Limit: 15 minutes	Practice #1	Practice #2	Practice #3	Final
10. Fill in the vendor's order form (or type a letter of request). Order by telephone, fax, e-mail, or online. Online ordering will expedite the order. Follow procedures that have been approved by the physician or office manager. When placing an order, have all the necessary information at hand, including the correct name of the item and the order and account numbers. Record the order information in the inventory file for that item. Be sure to obtain from the vendor an estimated arrival time for the order and mark that date and order number on your calendar.				
11. When ordering online, save the website to "Favorites" for easy, one-click future access. Select the website and establish an account with the company. To establish an account, you will need to give information about your office practice, including the name of the practice, contact name, the address, the phone number, an e-mail address, and a payment source. Ask about adding the practice to any special contact lists for promotional materials and discounts.				
12. When you receive the shipment, record the date and the amount received on the item's inventory card or record page. Check the shipment against the original order and the packing slip inside the package to ensure that the right items, sizes, styles, packaging, and amounts have arrived. If there is any error, immediately call or e-mail the vendor, with the catalog page and the inventory card or record page at hand.*				
13 Check the invoice carefully against the original order and the packing slip, making sure that the bill has not already been paid. Sign or stamp the invoice to show that the order was received.				
14. Write a check to the vendor to be signed by the physician. (Check writing procedures are described in Chapter 18.) Be sure to show the physician the original order, packing slip, and invoice. Record the check number, date, and amount of payment on the invoice and initial it or have the physician do so. Write the invoice number on the front of the check.*				
15. Mail the check and the vendor's copy of the invoice to the vendor within 30 days and file the office copy of the invoice with the original order and packing slip.				
Total Number of Points Achieved/Final Score				
Initials of Observer:				

Comments and Signatures

Reviewer's comments and signatures:

1. ______________________________

2. ______________________________

3. ______________________________

Instructor's comments:

____

Name ______________________ Class ______________ Date __________

CHAPTER 9

Maintaining Patient Records

Review

Vocabulary Review

True or False

Decide whether each statement is true or false. In the space at the left, write T *for true or* F *for false. On the lines provided, rewrite the false statements to make them true.*

_______ 1. It is not necessary to document in the medical record when a patient in noncompliant.

____

_______ 2. Patient records may be used to evaluate the quality of treatment a facility or doctor's office provides.

____

_______ 3. Informed consent forms state that a patient has agreed to treatment.

____

_______ 4. All written correspondence from the patient, a doctor's office, a laboratory, or an independent heath-care agency should be kept in the patient's chart.

____

_______ 5. When talking with an older patient, it is important to always speak very loudly as most older patients are hard of hearing.

____

_______ 6. Transcription is the transforming of written notes into accurate spoken form.

____

_______ 7. Problem-oriented medical records are a way to overcome the disadvantages of conventional medical charting.

____

_______ 8. Objective data comes from the physician and from exams and test results.

____

_______ 9. Computerized records can be used in teleconferences.

____

Name ________________________ Class ________________ Date ____________

Content Review

Multiple Choice

In the space provided, write the letter of the choice that best completes each statement or answers each question.

_______ **1.** When you are in doubt regarding who is authorized to sign a release of records form for a minor,

A. always ask the oldest person.

B. always ask the minor who is authorized.

C. do not allow anyone to sign.

D. you must ask a lawyer for guidance.

E. you must always ask your superior.

_______ **2.** When children reach this age, most states consider them adults with the right to privacy regarding all of their medical information.

A. 18

B. 19

C. 20

D. 21

_______ **3.** Test results received from sources outside the practice are best organized in sections within what part of the medical chart?

A. Laboratory and other test results

B. A special section in the chart especially for outside source material

C. The very front of the chart

D. The very back of the chart

_______ **4.** Which of the following elements of SOAP charting describes the data that comes directly from the patient?

A. S

B. O

C. A

D. P

_______ **5.** Which of the following elements of SOAP charting describes the course of treatment to be followed?

A. S

B. O

C. A

D. P

_______ **6.** What does the abbreviation PT mean?

A. Partial

B. Physical Therapy

C. Patient

D. Preoperative

E. Professional Tone

_______ **7.** The six Cs of charting include

A. Conformity, Clarity, Cleanliness, Conciseness, Chronological order, and Confidentiality

B. Conformity, Clarity, Completeness, Conciseness, Chronological order, and Creativity

C. Client's words, Clarity, Completeness, Conciseness, Chronological order, and Confidentiality

D. Client's words, Conformity, Cleanliness, Conciseness, Chronological order, and Confidentiality

E. Client's words, Clarity, Conciseness, Conformity, Chronological order, and Confidentiality

_____ **8.** Conventional records are
A. also called source-oriented records.
B. also called POMR records.
C. organized by problems of the patient.
D. especially easy for tracking a specific ailment in a patient.

_____ **9.** The P in SOAP documentation stands for
A. purpose.
B. procedures.
C. physical.
D. plan.

_____ **10.** As a general rule, if information is not documented,
A. it is not important.
B. it is not useful.
C. no one can prove that an event or procedure took place.
D. it is illegal.

_____ **11.** The S in SOAP documentation stands for
A. subjective.
B. serious.
C. sensitive.
D. statistics.

_____ **12.** Original documentation
A. is always selected instead of a copy to be given to the patient on request.
B. cannot be faxed.
C. legally belongs to the patient.
D. legally belongs to the physician and belongs in the patient's medical chart.

_____ **13.** Completeness in charting means
A. using the patient's exact words.
B. dating all entries into a chart.
C. not leaving out information.
D. using precise descriptions and accepted medical terminology.

_____ **14.** The first form used in initiating a patient record is the
A. informed consent form.
B. doctor's diagnosis form.
C. doctor's treatment form.
D. patient registration form.

_____ **15.** The term *noncompliant* means that the patient
A. does not understand.
B. does not hear well.
C. is not literate.
D. does not follow medical advice and direction.

_____ **16.** When speaking with an older patient,
A. show an interest in the patient as a person.
B. speak clearly.
C. be patient.
D. All of the above

Name ________________________ Class ________________ Date ____________

_______ 17. If a physician who is dictating speaks with an accent and you find it difficult to understand the dictation, you should

- **A.** state you don't understand and stop.
- **B.** ask others in the office if they understand the physician and ask them to take dictation.
- **C.** record the dictation.
- **D.** do the best you can.
- **E.** ask the physician to speak more slowly than normal.

Sentence Completion

In the space provided, write the word or phrase that best completes each sentence.

18. The patient's past medical history, family medical history, and social and occupational history are included in a part of the chart called the _______.

19. It is important to date and _______ every entry you put in the patient chart so that it is easy to tell which items the medical assistant enters and which items other people enter.

20. When filling out patient charts, it is important to record patients' _______, not your interpretation of them.

21. To make chart data more concise, medical workers use standard medical abbreviations, such as "patient got _______" instead of "patient got out of bed."

22. All information in a patient's chart is _______, to protect the patient's privacy.

23. In a conventional, or source-oriented, record, all the patient's problems and treatments are recorded on the same form in _______ order.

24. In problem-oriented medical record keeping, each _______ is listed separately, making it easier for the physician to track a patient's progress.

25. When documenting problems, you must be careful to distinguish between signs, which are external factors that can be seen and measured, and symptoms, which are _______ that can be felt only by the patient.

26. Because the _______ of information in a patient's chart is important, check all information carefully before entering it.

27. The doctor's transcribed notes for the patient's chart should be initialed by the _______.

28. _______ provide physicians with easy access to patient information no matter where they are.

29. _______ charting describes a patient's condition by the use of four letters. The letters describe what the patient says, what the medical personnel see, an evaluation of the problem, and a directive for care.

30. _______ in medical records are not uncommon but must be changed immediately.

18. ______________________

19. ______________________

20. ______________________

21. ______________________

22. ______________________

23. ______________________

24. ______________________

25. ______________________

26. ______________________

27. ______________________

28. ______________________

29. ______________________

30. ______________________

31. _______ means "to leave out."

32. _______ is the age at which most states consider an individual to be an adult.

33. To maintain patient _______, never discuss a patient's records, forward them to another office, fax them, or show them to anyone but the physician unless you have the patient's written permission to do so.

34. A _______ contains a record of the patient's history, information from the initial interview with the patient, all findings and results from physical exams, and any tests, x-rays, and other procedures.

35. In the _______, patient information is arranged according to who supplied the data—the patient, the doctor, a specialist, or someone else.

36. _______ means in the order of the date in which it occurred.

37. _______ means to be brief and to the point.

31. ______________________

32. ______________________

33. ______________________

34. ______________________

35. ______________________

36. ______________________

37. ______________________

Short Answer

Write the answer to each question on the lines provided.

38. Explain the difference between patient signs and symptoms. List three examples of each.

39. Describe why it is so important to use care when making corrections to medical charts.

40. List four additions that a physician might want to make to a patient's chart.

41. List five tips for fast and accurate transcription of a doctor's recorded dictation.

42. Describe the SOAP approach to medical record documentation.

13. List six common medical abbreviations that are difficult for you to remember.

14. List six types of data contained in a patient's records.

Critical Thinking

Write the answer to each question on the lines provided.

1. Why is it important to date every entry in the medical record?

2. Do you think the advantages of computerizing medical records outweigh the disadvantages? Explain.

3. What could happen if a medical record was subpoenaed to a court of law and the record was incomplete?

4. Why do medical records include notes of all telephone calls to and from a patient?

5. How do the rules of privacy for the release of a 15-year-old patient's medical records differ from the rules that apply to an 18-year-old's records?

Application

Follow the directions for the application.

1. Initiating a Patient Record

Work with two partners. Each of you should take turns being a medical assistant, a patient, and an observer/evaluator. Assume that this is the patient's first visit to the medical office.

a. Working together, create a model for a patient record. It must contain all the standard chart information, including forms for patient registration, patient medical history, and a physical exam. (You may use the forms shown in Figures 9-2 and 9-3 of the textbook as a guide.)

b. Have one partner play the role of the medical assistant and another partner play the role of a patient complaining of headaches. The third partner should act as the observer and evaluator. Have the medica assistant help the patient complete the patient registration form. Then have the medical assistant interview the patient and record the medical history, using standard abbreviations where appropriate, endin with a description of the patient's reason for the visit. The medical assistant should document any signs, symptoms, or other information the patient wishes to share.

c. Have the evaluator critique the interview and the documentation in the patient chart. The critique should take into account the accuracy of the documentation, the order in which the medical history wa taken, and the history's completeness. The evaluator should also note the medical assistant's ability to follow the six Cs of charting, including the correct use of medical abbreviations.

d. The medical assistant, the patient, and the observer should discuss the observer's comments, noting th strengths and weaknesses of the interview and the quality of the documentation.

e. Exchange roles and repeat the exercise with a new patient. Allow the student playing the patient to choose a different medical problem.

f. Exchange roles again so that each member of the team has an opportunity to play the interviewer, the patient, and the observer once.

2. Correcting a Patient Record

a. Using the same patient information as in the model for a patient record created in Application 1, make a correction to three different parts of the record. Pay special attention to Procedure 9.2. Each team member should take turns making three corrections each.

b. Ask your instructor to review each correction and comment on your work. There should be no blacking out or the use of white correction fluid. All corrections should be clear and neat. All corrections should be dated and initialed. Make sure you indicate the reason you made the correction.

Case Studies

Write your response to each case study on the lines provided.

Case 1

You accidentally throw out a sheet of a patient's medical chart. The trash has already been taken away, so there is no chance for you to get it back. You are new in the office, and you are afraid of losing your job if you tel the doctor what you have done. You remember the information that was on the sheet. You think you can easily rewrite it. What should you do?

____

____

____

Name ______________________ Class ______________ Date ___________

Case 2

The doctor you work for reads information about her patients into a tape recorder. You then must transcribe the information and enter it into patient charts. The doctor has a pronounced accent, and many of her words are difficult for you to understand. How should you handle the situation?

____

____

____

Case 3

A former patient of the doctor you work for calls and asks you to send her medical records to her new doctor. She says it is important that the records get to her new doctor by this afternoon and asks you to fax them. Would you have a problem with this request? Why or why not?

____

____

____

Case 4

Dr. Smith receives laboratory results from a test performed on Mr. Jones. He calls Mr. Jones at home on Monday, July 6, at 10:00 A.M. He gets no answer, but he leaves a message on Mr. Jones's answering machine asking him to call the office. By 10:00 A.M. the next morning, Dr. Smith has received no answer from Mr. Jones. He calls again and reaches Mrs. Jones and asks her to have her husband call the office. Mr. Jones calls the doctor's office at 2:30 that afternoon. Dr. Smith discusses the test results with Mr. Jones and asks him to make an appointment for the following week. Mr. Jones is connected with the receptionist. He makes an appointment for 11:00 A.M. on July 12. As a medical assistant, how would you record this series of events in Mr. Jones's chart?

____

____

____

Procedure Competency Checklists

Procedure 9.1 Preparing a Patient Medical Record/Chart

Procedure Goal

To assemble new patient record/charts

Scoring System

To score each step, use the following scoring system:
1 = poor, 2 = fair, 3 = good, 4 = excellent

A minimum score of at least a 3 must be achieved on **each** step to achieve successful completion of the technique. Detailed instructions on the scoring system are found on page x of the Preface.

Materials

File folder, labels as appropriate (alphabet, numbers, dates, insurance, allergies, etc.), forms (patient information, advance directives, physician progress notes, referrals, laboratory forms), hole punch

Name ______________________ Class ______________ Date __________

Procedure

Procedure Steps Total Possible Points - 24 Time Limit: 10 minutes	Practice #1	Practice #2	Practice #3	Final
1. Carefully create a chart label according to practice policy. This label may include the patient's last name followed by the first name, or it may be a medical record number for those offices that utilize numeric or alphanumeric filing.*				
2. Place the chart label on the right edge of the folder, extending the label the length of the tab on the folder.				
3. Place the date label on the top edge of the folder, updating the date according to the practice's policy. (The date is usually updated annually, provided the patient has come into the office within the last year.)*				
4. If alpha or numeric filing labels are utilized, place a patient name label on the chart according to the practice's policy.				
5. Punch holes in the appropriate forms for placement within the patient's medical record/chart.				
6. Place all the forms in appropriate sections of the patient's medical record/chart.				
Total Number of Points Achieved/Final Score				
Initials of Observer:				

Comments and Signatures

Reviewer's comments and signatures:

1. ______________________________

2. ______________________________

3. ______________________________

Instructor's comments:

____

Procedure 9.2 Correcting Medical Records

Procedure Goal

To follow standard procedures for correcting a medical record

Scoring System

To score each step, use the following scoring system:
1 = poor, 2 = fair, 3 = good, 4 = excellent

A minimum score of at least a 3 must be achieved on **each** step to achieve successful completion of the technique. Detailed instructions on the scoring system are found on page x of the Preface.

Name ________________ Class ________________ Date ________________

Materials

Patient file, other pertinent documents that contain the information to be used in making corrections (for example, transcribed notes, telephone notes, physician's comments, correspondence), good ballpoint pen

Procedure

Procedure Steps Total Possible Points - 24 Time Limit: 5 minutes	Practice #1	Practice #2	Practice #3	Final
1. Always make the correction in a way that does not suggest any intention to deceive, cover up, alter, or add information to conceal a lack of proper medical care.				
2. When deleting information, never black it out, never use correction fluid to cover it up, and never in any other way erase or obliterate the original wording. Draw a line through the original information so that it is still legible.*				
3. Write or type in the correct information above or below the original line or in the margin. The location on the chart for the new information should be clear. You may need to attach another sheet of paper or another document with the correction on it. Note in the record "See attached document A" or similar wording to indicate where the corrected information can be found.				
4. Place a note near the correction stating why it was made (for example, "error, wrong date; error, interrupted by phone call"). This indication can be a brief note in the margin or an attachment to the record. As a general rule of thumb, do not make any changes without noting the reason for them.*				
5. Enter the date and time and initial the correction.*				
6. If possible, have another staff member or the physician witness and initial the correction to the record when you make it.				
Total Number of Points Achieved/Final Score				
Initials of Observer:				

Comments and Signatures

Reviewer's comments and signatures:

1. ________________________________

2. ________________________________

3. ________________________________

Instructor's comments:

____

Name ______________________ Class ______________ Date ______________

Procedure 9.3 Maintaining Medical Records

Procedure Goal

To document continuity of care by creating a complete, accurate, timely record of the medical care provided at your facility

Scoring System

To score each step, use the following scoring system:
1 = poor, 2 = fair, 3 = good, 4 = excellent

A minimum score of at least a 3 must be achieved on **each** step to achieve successful completion of the technique. Detailed instructions on the scoring system are found on page x of the Preface.

Materials

Patient file, other pertinent documents (test results, x-rays, telephone notes, correspondence), blue ballpoint pen, notebook, keyboard, transcribing equipment

Procedure

Procedure Steps Total Possible Points - 40 Time Limit: 10 minutes	Practice #1	Practice #2	Practice #3	Final
1. Verify that you have the correct chart for the records to be filed.*				
2. Transcribe dictated doctor's notes as soon as possible and enter them into the patient record.*				
3. Spell out the names of disorders, diseases, medications, and other terms the first time you enter them into the patient record, followed by the appropriate abbreviation (for example: "congestive heart failure [CHF]"). Thereafter, you may use the abbreviation alone.*				
4. Enter only what the doctor has dictated. Do *not* add your own comments, observations, or evaluations. Use self-adhesive flags or other means to call the doctor's attention to something you have noticed that may be helpful to the patient's case. Date and initial each entry.*				
5. Follow office procedure to record routine or special laboratory test results. They may be posted in a particular section of the file or on a separate test summary form. If you use the summary form, make a note in the file that the results were received and recorded. Place the original laboratory report in the patient's file if required to do so by office policy. Date and initial each entry. Always note in the chart the date of the test and the results, whether or not test result printouts are filed in the record.				
6. Make a note in the record of all telephone calls to and from the patient. Date and initial the entries. These entries may also include the doctor's comments, observations, changes in the patient's medication, new instructions to the patient, and so on. If calls are recorded in a separate telephone log, note in the patient's record the time and date of the call and refer to the log. It is particularly important to record such calls when the patient resists or refuses treatment, skips appointments, or has not made follow-up appointments.*				

(continued)

Name ______________________ Class ______________ Date ____________

Procedure Steps Total Possible Points - 40 Time Limit: 10 minutes	Practice #1	Practice #2	Practice #3	Final
7. Read over the entries for omissions or mistakes. Ask the doctor to answer any questions you have.*				
8. Make sure that you have dated and initialed each entry.				
9. Be sure that all documents are included in the file.				
10. Replace the patient's file in the filing system as soon as possible.				
Total Number of Points Achieved/Final Score				
Initials of Observer:				

Comments and Signatures

Reviewer's comments and signatures:

1. ______________________________

2. ______________________________

3. ______________________________

Instructor's comments:

____

Name ______________________ Class ______________ Date __________

CHAPTER 10

Managing the Office Medical Records

REVIEW

Vocabulary Review

Matching

Match the key terms in the right column with the definitions in the left column by placing the letter of each correct answer in the space provided.

_______ 1. Pullout drawers in which hanging file folders are hung

_______ 2. Horizontal filing cabinets

_______ 3. Reminder files

_______ 4. Frequently used files

_______ 5. Infrequently used files

_______ 6. Files that are no longer consulted

a. inactive files
b. vertical files
c. active files
d. tickler files
e. lateral files
f. closed files

True or False

Decide whether each statement is true or false. In the space at the left, write T *for true or* F *for false. On the lines provided, rewrite the false statements to make them true.*

_______ 7. If storage space is limited, there are a number of paperless options for storing files.

____

_______ 8. No matter where you store files, you must consider the issue of safety as well as security.

____

_______ 9. The rules of indexing state that all hyphenated names are always considered to be one name.

____

_______ 10. HIPAA law requires that every covered entity have appropriate safeguards to ensure the protection of the patient's confidential health information.

____

_______ 11. Physicians must keep all immunization records on file in the office for 2 years.

____

_______ 12. In terminal digital filing, numbers are read from right to left.

____

_______ 13. Horizontal file cabinets are also called lateral file cabinets.

____

______ **14.** A records management system refers to the way patient records are created, filed, and maintained.

____

______ **15.** Commercial records centers manage stored documents for medical practices.

____

______ **16.** When inserting documents into folders already in place in the drawer, lift the folders up and out of the drawer.

____

______ **17.** You should write the name of a patient on the tab of a file folder.

____

______ **18.** It is not important to use a file guide as a placeholder to indicate that a file has been taken out of the filing system.

____

______ **19.** The final step in the filing process is to store the files in the appropriate filing equipment.

____

______ **20.** In an alphabetic filing system, files are placed in alphabetic order according to the patients' last names.

____

______ **21.** Many legal consultants advise that doctors maintain patient records for at least 7 years to protect themselves against malpractice suits.

____

______ **22.** A file that has been cross-referenced has been placed in more than one location.

____

______ **23.** The American Medical Association, the American Hospital Association, and other groups generally suggest that doctors keep patient records for up to 10 years after a patient's final visit or contact.

____

______ **24.** *Indexing* is another term for naming a file.

____

Content Review

Multiple Choice

In the space provided, write the letter of the choice that best completes each statement or answers each question.

______ **1.** If you are unsure whether to cross-reference a file, the best policy is

A. to not do it.
B. to do it.
C. to let someone else make the decision.
D. to not put the file away. Set the file on your desk.
E. to place the unlabeled file into the file cabinet or filing system.

_______ **2.** A numeric filing system

A. is not used when patient confidentiality is especially important.
B. organizes records according to the patient's last name.
C. may include numbers that indicate where in the filing system a file can be found.
D. is the only practical system for a large practice.

_______ **3.** Use color-coding for files

A. only when using a numeric filing system.
B. to identify files belonging to specific categories of patients.
C. only when you are using no other filing system.
D. to reduce the risk of misplacing files.

_______ **4.** For tickler files to work effectively, they must be

A. kept in file folders.
B. kept in a file box
C. listed on a calendar
D. placed in the computer.
E. checked frequently.

_______ **5.** The *first* step in locating a misplaced file is to

A. look for the color of the misfiled chart.
B. discuss it with the person in charge of the office.
C. check the doctor's office to see if it is on her desk.
D. check with the other employees.
E. determine the last time you knew the file's location.

_______ **6.** The medical records for patients who have died should be placed in which type of file?

A. Active
B. Inactive
C. Closed
D. Reserved

_______ **7.** When files are organized in a variety of filing systems that place patient records one after the other in a pattern or an order, it is referred to as a

A. sequential order.
B. labeled order.
C. tabbed order.
D. standard order.

_______ **8.** A new patient is

A. always an infant.
B. a patient who has never been seen in the practice before.
C. a patient who has never been seen in the practice before or has not been seen by a physician in the same specialty in the practice in 3 years.
D. never a patient who transferred from another practice.

_______ **9.** To make the best use of a color filing system, you must

A. use only bright colors.
B. use no more than 4 colors.
C. always color-code a file based on the age of the patient.
D. first identify the classifications that are important in your office.
E. never combine a color-coding system with any other filing system.

_______ 10. Filing guidelines
- A. help you file more efficiently.
- B. help you select a filing system.
- C. identify who is responsible for all filing.
- D. help you set up a tickler system.

_______ 11. When selecting a commercial records center to assist with patient records, it is important to
- A. assess the monthly fee.
- B. assess the location.
- C. assess the system for retrieval and delivery of files.
- D. All of the above

_______ 12. Who can take an original patient medical record out of the medical office?
- A. The office manager
- B. The medical assistant
- C. The nurse
- D. No one
- E. The patient

_______ 13. The proper order for the steps of filing is
- A. sort, inspect, code, index, and store.
- B. store, inspect, index, code, and sort.
- C. inspect, index, code, sort, and store.
- D. index, inspect, code, sort, and store.

_______ 14. Rotary circular files
- A. take up a lot of room and should only be used in a spacious office.
- B. can only be operated manually.
- C. are a good option when space is limited.
- D. can only be operated electronically.
- E. can be stored stacked on top of one another.

Sentence Completion

In the space provided, write the word or phrase that best completes each sentence.

15. Vertical files have a metal frame from which _______ are hung.
16. _______ can be skipped when filing patient records that have been previously filed.
17. To protect the confidentiality of patient records, always keep them in a(n) _______ area.
18. _______ are large envelope-style folders with tabs in which files can be stored temporarily.
19. When a record is filed in two or more places, it is _______.
20. If you need to keep some patient-related materials separate from the patient's medical record, you should create a(n) _______ file.
21. _______ is another term for naming a file.
22. When you put an identifying mark or phrase on a document to ensure that it is properly filed, you _______ it.

15. ______________________
16. ______________________
17. ______________________
18. ______________________
19. ______________________
20. ______________________
21. ______________________
22. ______________________

Name ______________________ Class ______________ Date ______________

23. Placing files in a pattern or sequence is referred to as ________. 23. ______________

Short Answer

Write the answer to each question on the lines provided.

24. Why is it important to completely remove a file from the drawer in order to file correctly?

25. When small documents have wording on both sides of the paper, how should they be filed?

26. What are two safety concerns when using filing equipment?

27. What is the purpose of the tabs on file folders, and why are they positioned in different places on the folders?

28. What is the purpose of the pockets on some out guides?

29. You should choose file guides with a different tab position than your folders to help them stand out. How far apart should you position guides?

30. Name the five steps in the filing process.

31. List four formats in which inactive and closed files can be stored.

Name ______________________ Class ______________ Date ____________

32. Name and describe in detail the first step in filing.

33. Why is it important to post a written copy of the practice retention policy near the filing area?

34. Describe how supplemental files are different from primary medical records.

35. Describe the "Indexing" step in filing. What is included?

36. Describe the steps to follow if a file is misplaced.

Critical Thinking

Write the answer to each question on the lines provided.

1. Why is it important not to misplace patient files?

2. What are some of the things that could possibly occur as a result of a medical file being lost?

3. What filing system would you choose for a practice that has many patients who are celebrities? Explain.

4. How can color-coded patient files be helpful in the care and treatment of patients who have illnesses such as diabetes or HIV?

5. Who might be impacted when a medical file is mismanaged or lost?

Application

Follow the directions for each application.

1. **Creating a Patient Filing System**

   Work in groups of four students. Within your group, choose partners to work together.

   a. With your partner, prepare a list of 15 hypothetical patients—complete with full names, ages, and primary ailments. Exchange patient lists with the other pair of students in your group.

   b. With your partner, analyze the patient list you have been given. Determine what kind of filing system, alphabetic or numeric, is appropriate.

   c. Organize the patients' names as you would for the filing system you have chosen. If you have chosen the alphabetic system, write each name on a different index card and organize the cards. If you have chosen the numeric system, create a master list that shows the numbers and the corresponding patient names.

   d. Assume that your patient list is part of a much larger filing system that contains a similar mix of patients. Color-code your filing system. With your partner, decide what categories of information you need to identify through color-coding. Then assign colors to your patient list as appropriate.

   e. After you have completed your filing system, meet with the other pair of students in your group and compare filing systems. How are they different? How are they alike? Each pair should evaluate the other pair's filing system for appropriateness and accuracy. Pairs should be able to justify their choices.

   f. Form different groups of four students. Exchange your original patient list with a different pair of students and repeat steps **b** through **e.**

2. **Setting Up a Tickler File**

   Work with two partners. Two of you are medical assistants in charge of setting up a tickler file. The third partner is an evaluator.

   a. On the chalkboard, each student in the class should list one important date or activity that he needs to be reminded of weekly, monthly, or annually.

   b. Working together, the two medical assistants should analyze the reminder information to be included in the tickler file. Decide how you will organize the tickler file. Will you use file folders, a wall chart, a calendar, a binder, or a computer file? Create the tickler file.

   c. Have the evaluator critique the tickler file. Her critique should answer these questions: Has any information been overlooked, misplaced, or duplicated? Is the tickler file accurate? Will it help in the day-to-day workings of an office?

Name ______________________ Class ______________ Date __________

d. As a group, discuss the evaluator's comments, noting the strengths and weaknesses of the tickler file as well as its accuracy and completeness.

e. Exchange roles and repeat the activity, choosing a different way of organizing the tickler file.

f. Exchange roles again so that each member of the group has an opportunity to set up and evaluate a tickler file.

Case Studies

Write your response to each case study on the lines provided.

Case 1

You are in charge of the patient filing system for an office with four doctors. The system seems efficient, except that there is no way of knowing who has removed a particular file. You have had to go on numerous searches for missing files only to find them on someone's desk. What change could you make to the system to reduce the need to search the office for missing files?

____

____

____

Case 2

You have a new job. On your first day you learn that no one has filed in weeks. Medical records are stacked on the floor. No one in the office can find what they need and the physicians are complaining. You are told that there are at least two lost records. What do you do?

____

____

____

Case 3

You have noticed that the patient files in your office contain medical records going back many years. It is becoming increasingly difficult to sort through all the documents and locate current medical information in a file. What can be done to solve this problem?

____

____

____

Case 4

Your medical office stores all inactive medical records in cardboard boxes in an area next to the furnace and hot water heater. The boxes are stacked on top of each other in tightly packed rows. The boxes are numbered but it is not possible to read the numbering because there are so many boxes in the small room. The boxes are sitting directly on the floor and are stacked almost to the ceiling. What suggestions would you make to improve this situation?

____

____

____

Name ______________________________ Class ____________________ Date ____________

Procedure Competency Checklists

PROCEDURE 10.1 CREATING A FILING SYSTEM FOR PATIENT RECORDS

Procedure Goal

To create a filing system that keeps related materials together in a logical order and enables office staff to store and retrieve files efficiently

Scoring System

To score each step, use the following scoring system:
1 = poor, 2 = fair, 3 = good, 4 = excellent

A minimum score of at least a 3 must be achieved on **each** step to achieve successful completion of the technique. Detailed instructions on the scoring system are found on page x of the Preface.

Materials

Vertical or horizontal filing cabinets with locks, file jackets, tabbed file folders, labels, file guides, out guides, filing sorters

Procedure

Procedure Steps Total Possible Points - 32 Time Limit: 15 minutes	Practice #1	Practice #2	Practice #3	Final
1. Evaluate which filing system is best for your office—alphabetic or numeric. Make sure the doctor approves the system you choose.*				
2. Establish a style for labeling files and make sure that all file labels are prepared in this manner. Place records for different family members in separate files.				
3. Avoid writing labels by hand. Use a keyboard, a label maker, or preprinted adhesive labels.				
4. Set up a color-coding system to distinguish the files (for example, use blue for the letters A–C, red for D–F, and so on). Create a chart, suitable to be hung in a professional file room, that indicates the color-coding system.				
5. Use file guides to divide files into sections.				
6. Use out- guides as placeholders to indicate which files have been taken out of the system. Include a charge-out form to be signed and dated by the person who is taking the file.*				
7. To keep files in order and to prevent them from being misplaced, use a file sorter to hold those patient records that will be returned to the files during the day or at the end of the day.				
8. Develop a manual explaining the filing system to new staff members. Include guidelines on how to keep the system in good order.				

(continued)

Name ______________________ Class ______________ Date ____________

Procedure Steps Total Possible Points - 32 Time Limit: 15 minutes	Practice #1	Practice #2	Practice #3	Final
Total Number of Points Achieved/Final Score				
Initials of Observer:				

Comments and Signatures

Reviewer's comments and signatures:

1. ______________________

2. ______________________

3. ______________________

Instructor's comments:

____

Procedure 10.2 Setting Up an Office Tickler File

Procedure Goal

To create a comprehensive office tickler file designed for year-round use

Scoring System

To score each step, use the following scoring system:
1 = poor, 2 = fair, 3 = good, 4 = excellent
A minimum score of at least a 3 must be achieved on **each** step to achieve successful completion of the technique. Detailed instructions on the scoring system are found on page x of the Preface.

Materials

12 manila file folders, 12 file labels, pen or typewriter, paper

Procedure

Procedure Steps Total Possible Points - 40 Time Limit: 15 minutes	Practice #1	Practice #2	Practice #3	Final
1. Write or type twelve file labels, one for each month of the year. Abbreviations are acceptable. Do *not* include the current calendar year, just the month.				
2. Affix one label to the tab of each file folder.				
3. Arrange the folders so that the current month is on the top of the pile. Months should follow in chronological order.				
4. Write or type a list of upcoming responsibilities and activities. Next to each activity, indicate the date by which the activity should be completed. Leave a column after this date to indicate when the activity has been completed. Use a separate sheet of paper for each month.*				

(continued)

Name ______________________ Class ______________ Date __________

Procedure Steps Total Possible Points - 40 Time Limit: 15 minutes	Practice #1	Practice #2	Practice #3	Final
5. File the notes by month in the appropriate folders.*				
6. Place the folders, with the current month on top, in order, in a prominent place in the office, such as in a plastic box mounted on the wall near the receptionist's desk.				
7. Check the tickler file at least once a week on a specific day, such as every Monday. Assign a backup person to check it in case you happen to be out of the office.				
8. Complete the tickler activities on the designated days, if possible. Keep notes concerning activities in progress. Be sure to note when activities are completed and by whom.*				
9. At the end of the month, place that month's file folder at the bottom of the tickler file. If there are notes remaining in that month's folder, move them to the new month's folder.*				
10. Continue to add new notes to the appropriate tickler files.*				
Total Number of Points Achieved/Final Score				
Initials of Observer:				

Comments and Signatures

Reviewer's comments and signatures:

1. ______________________________

2. ______________________________

3. ______________________________

Instructor's comments:

____

Procedure 10.3 Developing a Records Retention Program

Procedure Goal

To establish a records retention program for patient medical records that meets office needs as well as legal and government guidelines

Scoring System

To score each step, use the following scoring system:
1 = poor, 2 = fair, 3 = good, 4 = excellent

A minimum score of at least a 3 must be achieved on **each** step to achieve successful completion of the technique. Detailed instructions on the scoring system are found on page x of the Preface.

Materials

Updated guide for record retention as described by federal and state law (go to the HIPAA Advisory website), file folders, index cards, index box, paper, pen or typewriter

Name ______________________ Class ______________ Date __________

Procedure

Procedure Steps Total Possible Points - 48 Time Limit: 20 minutes	Practice #1	Practice #2	Practice #3	Final
1. List the types of information contained in a typical patient medical record in your office. For example, a file for an adult patient may include the patient's case history, records of hospital stays, and insurance information.				
2. Research the state and federal requirements for keeping documents. Contact your appropriate state office (such as the office of the insurance commissioner) for specific state requirements, such as rules for keeping records of insurance payments and the statute of limitations for initiating lawsuits. If your office does business in more than one state, be sure to research all applicable regulations. Consult with the attorney who represents your practice.				
3. Compile the results of your research in a chart. At the top of the chart, list the different kinds of information your office keeps in patient records. Down the left side of the chart, list the headings "Federal," "State," and "Other." Then, in each box, record the corresponding information.				
4. Compare all the legal and government requirements. Indicate which one is for the longest period of time.*				
5. Meet with the doctor to review the information. Working together with the physician, prepare a retention schedule. Determine how long different types of patient records should be kept in the office after a patient leaves the practice and how long records should be kept in storage. Although retention periods can vary based on the type of information kept in a file, it is often easiest to choose a retention period that covers all records. For example, all records could be kept in the office for 1 year after a patient leaves the practice and then kept in storage for another 9 years, for a total of 10 years. Determine how files will be destroyed when they have exceeded the retention requirements. Usually, records are destroyed by paper shredding. Purchase the appropriate equipment, or contract with a shredding company as necessary.*				
6. Put the retention schedule in writing and post it prominently near the files. In addition, keep a copy of the schedule in a safe place in the office. Review it with the office staff.				
7. Develop a system for identifying files easily under the retention system. For example, for each file deemed inactive or closed, prepare an index card or create a master list containing the following information: • Patient's name and Social Security number • Contents of the file				

(continued)

Name ______________________ Class ______________ Date __________

Procedure Steps Total Possible Points - 48 Time Limit: 20 minutes	Practice #1	Practice #2	Practice #3	Final
• Date the file was deemed inactive or closed and by whom • Date the file should be sent to inactive or closed file storage (the actual date will be filled in later; if more than one storage location is used, indicate the exact location to which the file was sent) • Date the file should be destroyed (the actual date will be filled in later) Have the card signed by the doctor and by the person responsible for the files. Keep the card in an index box or another safe place. This is your authorization to destroy the file at the appropriate time.				
8. Use color-coding to help identify inactive and closed files. For example, all records that become inactive in 2008 could be placed in green file folders or have a green sticker with 08 placed on them and moved to a supplemental file. Then, in January 2010, all of these files could be pulled and sent to storage.				
9. One person should be responsible for checking the index cards once a month to determine which stored files should be destroyed. Before retrieving these files from storage, circulate a notice to the office staff stating which records will be destroyed. Indicate that the staff must let you know by a specific date if any of the files should be saved. You may want to keep a separate file with these notices.				
10. After the deadline has passed, retrieve the files from storage. Review each file before it is destroyed. Make sure the staff members who will destroy the files are trained to use the equipment properly. Develop a sheet of instructions for destroying files. Post it prominently with the retention schedule, near the machinery used to destroy the files.*				
11. Update the index card, giving the date the file was destroyed and by whom.				
12. Periodically review the retention schedule. Update it with the most current legal and governmental requirements. With the staff, evaluate whether the current schedule is meeting the needs of your office or whether files are being kept too long or destroyed prematurely. With the doctor's approval, change the schedule as necessary.				

(continued)

Name ______________________ Class ______________ Date __________

Procedure Steps Total Possible Points - 48 Time Limit: 20 minutes	Practice #1	Practice #2	Practice #3	Final
Total Number of Points Achieved/Final Score				
Initials of Observer:				

Comments and Signatures

Reviewer's comments and signatures:

1. ______________________________

2. ______________________________

3. ______________________________

Instructor's comments:

____

Name ______________________ Class ______________ Date __________

CHAPTER 11

Telephone Techniques

REVIEW

Vocabulary Review

Matching

Match the key terms in the right column with the definitions in the left column by placing the letter of each correct answer in the space provided.

_______ **1.** screening a call

_______ **2.** HIPAA

_______ **3.** incoming calls

_______ **4.** example of courtesy

_______ **5.** enunciation

_______ **6.** routing list

_______ **7.** telephone answering system

_______ **8.** documenting

_______ **9.** ARU telephone system

_______ **10.** tone

a. speaking in a positive, respectful manner
b. calls made to the medical office
c. writing in the patient's chart
d. telecommunication
e. concerned with privacy and confidentiality
f. apologizing for delays or errors
g. specifies who is responsible for various types of calls and how the calls are to be handled
h. automated voicemail system
i. determining the need of the caller
j. clear and distinct speaking

Passage Completion

Study the key terms in the box. Use your textbook to find definitions of terms you do not understand.

enunciation	pitch	telephone triage
etiquette	pronunciation	

Name ______________________________ Class ____________________ Date ______________

In the space provided, complete the following passage, using the terms from the box. You may change the form of a term to fit the meaning of the sentence.

The telephone is an important tool in today's medical practice. How you handle telephone calls will have an impact on the public image of the office. When speaking on the telephone, always use proper telephone (11) _______ to present a positive impression of the office. Make your voice pleasant and effective by varying your (12) _______. Remember not to mumble. Good (13) _______ will help the caller understand the important information you are trying to convey. Proper (14) _______ of the caller's name will help her feel welcome and important. In today's medical practice, the process of determining the level of urgency of each call and how it should be handled or routed is called (15) _______.

11. ______________________________

12. ______________________________

13. ______________________________

14. ______________________________

15. ______________________________

Content Review

Multiple Choice

In the space provided, write the letter of the choice that best completes each statement or answers each question.

_______ **1.** When checking for understanding during a call,
- **A.** watch for visual signals.
- **B.** ask the caller if there are any questions.
- **C.** repeat everything at least twice.
- **D.** ask the caller to explain the information to a third person.

_______ **2.** The correct use of a telephone log includes
- **A.** keeping 3 copies of each phone message.
- **B.** keeping 2 copies of each phone message.
- **C.** using only a spiral-bound book.
- **D.** using only a message pad.
- **E.** giving the original message to the appropriate person and retaining a copy.

_______ **3.** If a caller refuses to discuss his symptoms with anyone but the physician,
- **A.** schedule an appointment immediately.
- **B.** try to talk the patient into talking with you.
- **C.** have the doctor return the call.
- **D.** call the patient the next day to see whether he has changed his mind.

_______ **4.** A fax machine
- **A.** should never be used to send a patient referral.
- **B.** is confidential.
- **C.** uses a phone line.
- **D.** is inappropriate for use in a medical practice.
- **E.** is a type of telephone routing system.

_______ **5.** An automated telecommunications system
- **A.** is inappropriate for use in a medical practice.
- **B.** is used in many hospitals and ambulatory care settings.
- **C.** is more expensive than using a phone operator.
- **D.** requires that the caller know exactly who he wants to speak to.

_______ **6.** What is the best way to deal with salespeople in a medical office?

A. On the telephone, ask the salesperson to send information about new products and services.

B. Do not speak to salespeople on the phone at all. Just hang up.

C. Allow salespeople to meet with the doctor between patients based on how long they have had to wait.

D. Medical assistants do not deal with salespeople in person or on the phone. That is the role of the doctor.

_______ **7.** A patient calls and tells you he is having severe vomiting. What should you do?

A. Make an appointment for the next day.

B. Immediately put the call through to a doctor or handle the call according to the established office procedures for patients that need immediate medical help.

C. Make an appointment for the patient within the next 3 days.

D. Make an appointment for an annual physical exam.

_______ **8.** If you are in doubt about whether a situation is a medical emergency,

A. you should treat it like an emergency.

B. you can ignore the situation if the patient tells you he does not want to see the doctor.

C. you should ask the patient to sit down so he can be observed.

D. you should rely on your intuition to do the right thing.

_______ **9.** A medical assistant may release patient information to an outside caller

A. only when requested to do so by the physician.

B. only when that caller is a physician.

C. only when that caller is an attorney.

D. whenever it is requested.

_______ **10.** Pronunciation is

A. the high or low level of speech.

B. the pitch of the voice.

C. the tone of the voice.

D. saying words correctly.

E. speaking without any accent.

_______ **11.** The best way to hold a telephone when you are using it is

A. with one hand.

B. with a telephone rest.

C. propped on your shoulder so you have both hands free.

D. propped on your shoulder, making sure you change shoulders every 3 minutes to avoid fatigue.

E. Both A and B

_______ **12.** Telephone triage

A. is the screening and sorting of emergency incidents over the phone.

B. is only done by RNs.

C. is an automatic message that is easily programmed into an automatic router.

D. means diagnosing the patient over the phone.

_______ **13.** How do you properly respond to a patient who is asking for the results of a lab test?

A. Tell the patient the results.

B. Never tell the patient anything.

C. Tell the patient the results only when the results are normal.

D. Follow the policies of the medical office.

______ **14.** If a patient remains dissatisfied after discussing a bill,
- **A.** document all comments and relay the information to the physician.
- **B.** tell the patient that you are sorry he is dissatisfied, but the bill stands as is.
- **C.** turn the patient's bill over to a collection agency.
- **D.** terminate the patient's care until the bill is paid.

______ **15.** How should a medical assistant respond to patient complaints?
- **A.** Listen carefully but never admit mistakes.
- **B.** Defend the doctor and the policies of the practice.
- **C.** Be careful to only raise your voice when the patient raises his voice.
- **D.** Acknowledge the patient's anger.
- **E.** Do not allow the patient to talk down to you.

Sentence Completion

In the space provided, write the word or phrase that best completes each sentence.

16. The medical assistant handles calls that deal with ______ issues.

17. ______ is a medical emergency in which there is a drop in body temperature during prolonged exposure to cold.

18. If you will be discussing clinical matters over the telephone, it is a good idea to pull the ______.

19. Never release any patient information to an outside caller unless the ______ asks you to.

20. The medical assistant may be responsible for making routine ______ to verify that patients are following treatment instructions.

21. ______ is clear and distinct speaking.

22. Before ending a telephone call, it is good professional behavior to always ______ the important points of the conversation.

23. Keeping a ______ on the desk allows you to easily find frequently used telephone numbers.

24. When taking a telephone message, always record the date and ______ of the call.

25. ______ is a medical emergency in which the patient experiences paleness, feeling faint, and a weak, rapid pulse.

16. ______
17. ______
18. ______
19. ______
20. ______
21. ______
22. ______
23. ______
24. ______
25. ______

Short Answer

Write the answer to each question on the lines provided.

26. List the features of good communications skills.

______
______
______

27. List three types of calls that a medical assistant would handle.

28. List the steps in calling in a prescription refill to a pharmacy.

29. List three types of incoming calls.

30. List at least ten symptoms or conditions that would qualify as a medical emergency.

31. What are five ways you can make your telephone voice effective?

32. What is the typical procedure for putting a call on hold?

33. How is telephone triage conducted?

Critical Thinking

Write the answer to each question on the lines provided.

1. How can the telephone image you present have an impact on public perception of your medical office?

Name ______________________ Class ______________ Date __________

2. Describe how you might handle a caller who is not a patient in the practice and who wants a prescription.

____

____

____

3. Describe how a medical assistant might respond when a patient calls the office to discuss symptoms she is experiencing.

____

____

____

4. If a patient calls with an emergency situation and can only stay on the telephone for 1 minute, what questions would be the most important to ask?

____

____

____

5. Discuss what you should do if you do not know how to respond to a caller's question on the phone.

____

____

____

6. The physician requests that you contact a patient and ask him to come in for an appointment, but the patient refuses to come in. What do you do?

____

____

____

7. Discuss how you would respond to a patient who calls to request a prescription refill.

____

____

____

8. Discuss guidelines for dealing with an angry caller.

____

____

____

Name ______________________________ Class ____________________ Date ____________

Application

Follow the directions for each application.

1. **Handling a Patient Call**

Work with two partners. Have one partner play the role of an angry patient calling to complain about being billed for a procedure that never took place. Have the second partner act as a medical assistant handling the call. Have the third partner act as an observer and evaluator.

a. Role-play the telephone call. The medical assistant should listen carefully to the caller, taking notes about the details of the problem. The medical assistant should also be sure to ask all necessary questions.

b. The medical assistant should respond to the caller's complaint in a professional manner and explain the specific action that will be taken to address the issue.

c. Have the observer provide a critique of the medical assistant's handling of the call. The critique should evaluate the use of proper telephone etiquette, the proper routing of the call, and the assistant's telephone notes. Comments should include both positive feedback and suggestions for improvement.

d. Exchange roles and repeat the exercise. Allow the student playing the caller to choose another reason for the call.

e. Exchange roles again so that each member of the group has an opportunity to play the role of the medical assistant.

f. Discuss the strengths and weaknesses of each group member's telephone etiquette.

2. **Taking Telephone Messages**

Work with a partner to design the best possible telephone message pad or telephone log for a medical office.

a. Consider the various types of incoming calls that the medical practice receives. Review the different types of information that a person taking a message might need to obtain. Make a list of the types of calls and types of information. Think about the order in which the information is obtained. Decide how much space is needed for each entry.

b. Choose which you will design—a telephone message pad or telephone log. As you work with your partner to design it, consider these questions: What is the best size for the pad or log? How many messages will fit on one page? How will copies be made? What color will the pad or log be? Pay attention to the information that must be included, the space available for each message, and the layout of the page.

c. Test your telephone message pad or log. Have your partner role-play a patient calling a medical office. Use your message pad or log to take the message.

d. Then trade roles and repeat the role playing. Discuss the strengths and weaknesses of your message pad or log. Revise your design as needed.

e. Share your message pad or log with other pairs of students. Critique each other's designs. Discuss how the designs are different and how they are similar. Assess the strengths and weaknesses of each design. Offer suggestions for revisions.

f. Make final adjustments to the design of your telephone message pad or telephone log on the basis of your classmates' feedback.

Name ______________________ Class ______________ Date __________

Case Studies

Write your response to each case study on the lines provided.

Case 1

You overhear another medical assistant speaking rudely to a patient. What should you do?

Case 2

A salesperson is continually calling on the telephone at the busiest time of day, tying up the line that is used to take patient calls. How might you handle the situation?

Case 3

In one morning, you receive calls from a patient with an emergency, an attorney, a physician from another medical office, and a salesperson. Describe how you would route each of these calls.

Case 4

A patient calls and says that he thinks he is having a heart attack. What do you do?

Case 5

Mrs. Rosetti calls the office and discusses a confidential medical problem with you. How should you handle this situation?

Case 6

A physician calls and asks to speak to the physician in your practice. The physician is with a patient. What do you do?

Name ______________________ Class ______________ Date ____________

Procedure Competency Checklists

PROCEDURE 11.1 CALLING A PRESCRIPTION REFILL INTO A PHARMACY

Procedure Goal

To accurately and efficiently place a telephone call to a pharmacy to refill a patient's prescription

Scoring System

To score each step, use the following scoring system:
1 = poor, 2 = fair, 3 = good, 4 = excellent

A minimum score of at least a 3 must be achieved on **each** step to achieve successful completion of the technique. Detailed instructions on the scoring system are found on page x of the Preface.

Materials

Patient chart with written order or prescription with the following information: the name of the drug, the drug dosage, the frequency and mode of administration, the number of refills authorized, and the name and phone number of the pharmacy

Procedure

Procedure Steps Total Possible Points - 48 Time Limit: 10 minutes	Practice #1	Practice #2	Practice #3	Final
1. Gather all materials and information necessary, checking for the doctor's written order (or prescription) in the chart. Seek clarification as needed. Schedule II and III drugs cannot be filled by a telephone order (refer to Chapter 50 for more information).*				
2. Follow your office policy regarding refills. Typically, refills are called in the day they are received. An example policy may be posted at the facility and may state: "Nonemergency prescription refill requests must be made during regular business hours. Please allow 24 hours for processing."				
3. Communicate the policy to the patient. You should know the policy and the time when the refills will be reviewed. For example, you might state, "Dr. Alexander will review the prescription between patients and it will be telephoned within one hour to the pharmacy. I will call you back if there is a problem."*				
4. Obtain the patient's chart or reference the electronic chart to verify you have the correct patient and that the patient is currently taking the medication. Check the patient's list of medications, which are usually part of the chart.				
5. Telephone the pharmacy. Identify yourself by name, the practice name, and the doctor's name.*				

(continued)

Name ________________________ Class ________________ Date ____________

Procedure Steps Total Possible Points - 48 Time Limit: 10 minutes	Practice #1	Practice #2	Practice #3	Final
6. State the purpose of the call. (Example: "I am calling to request a prescription refill for a patient.")				
7. Identify the patient. Include the patient's name, date of birth, address, and phone number.*				
8. Identify the drug (spelling the name when necessary), the dosage, the frequency and mode of administration, and any other special instructions or changes for administration (such as "take at bedtime").*				
9. State the number of refills authorized.				
10. If leaving a message on a pharmacy voicemail system set up for physicians, state your name, the name of the doctor you represent, and your phone number before you hang up.*				
11. Document the entire process in the patient's medical chart. Sign and date the entry per office policy.				
12. File the chart appropriately.				
Total Number of Points Achieved/Final Score				
Initials of Observer:				

Comments and Signatures

Reviewer's comments and signatures:

1. ____

2. ____

3. ____

Instructor's comments:

____

Procedure 11.2 Handling Emergency Calls

Procedure Goal

To determine whether a telephone call involves a medical emergency and to learn the steps to take if it is an emergency call

Scoring System

To score each step, use the following scoring system:
1 = poor, 2 = fair, 3 = good, 4 = excellent

A minimum score of at least a 3 must be achieved on **each** step to achieve successful completion of the technique. Detailed instructions on the scoring system are found on page x of the Preface.

Name ______________________ Class ______________ Date __________

Materials

Office guidelines for handling emergency calls; list of symptoms and conditions requiring immediate medical attention; telephone numbers of area emergency rooms, poison control centers, and ambulance transport services; telephone message forms or telephone message log

Procedure

Procedure Steps Total Possible Points - 32 Time Limit: 10 minutes	Practice #1	Practice #2	Practice #3	Final
1. When someone calls the office regarding a potential emergency, remain calm.*				
2. Obtain the following information, taking accurate notes: a. The caller's name b. The caller's telephone number and the address from which the call is being made* c. The caller's relationship to the patient (if it is not the patient who is calling) d. The patient's name (if the patient is not the caller) e. The patient's age f. A complete description of the patient's symptoms g. If the call is about an accident, a description of how the accident or injury occurred and any other pertinent information h. A description of how the patient is reacting to the situation i. Treatment that has been administered				
3. Read back the details of the medical problem to verify them.*				
4. If necessary, refer to the list of symptoms and conditions that require immediate medical attention to determine if the situation is indeed a medical emergency.				
If the Situation Is a Medical Emergency:				
1. Put the call through to the doctor immediately or handle the situation according to the established office procedures.*				
2. If the doctor is not in the office, follow established office procedures. They may involve one or more of the following: a. Transferring the call to the nurse practitioner or other medical personnel, as appropriate b. Instructing the caller to hang up and dial 911 to request an ambulance for the patient c. Instructing the patient to be driven to the nearest emergency room d. Instructing the caller to telephone the nearest poison control center for advice and supplying the caller with its telephone number e. Paging the doctor				
If the Situation Is Not a Medical Emergency:				
1. Handle the call according to established office procedures.				
2. If you are in doubt about whether the situation is a medical emergency, treat it like an emergency. You must always alert the doctor immediately about an emergency call, even if the patient declines to speak with the doctor.*				

(continued)

Name ______________________ Class ______________ Date __________

Procedure Steps Total Possible Points - 32 Time Limit: 10 minutes	Practice #1	Practice #2	Practice #3	Final
Total Number of Points Achieved/Final Score				
Initials of Observer:				

Comments and Signatures

Reviewer's comments and signatures:

1. ______________________________

2. ______________________________

3. ______________________________

Instructor's comments:

____

PROCEDURE 11.3 RETRIEVING MESSAGES FROM AN ANSWERING SERVICE

Procedure Goal

To follow standard procedures for retrieving messages from an answering service

Scoring System

To score each step, use the following scoring system:
1 = poor, 2 = fair, 3 = good, 4 = excellent

A minimum score of at least a 3 must be achieved on **each** step to achieve successful completion of the technique. Detailed instructions on the scoring system are found on page x of the Preface.

Materials

Telephone message pad, manual telephone log, or electronic telephone log

Procedure

Procedure Steps Total Possible Points - 24 Time Limit: 10 minutes	Practice #1	Practice #2	Practice #3	Final
1. Set a regular schedule for calling the answering service to retrieve messages.*				
2. Call at the regularly scheduled time(s) to see if there are any messages.				
3. Identify yourself and state that you are calling to obtain messages for the practice.*				
4. For each message, write down all pertinent information on the telephone message pad or telephone log or key it into the electronic telephone log. Be sure to include the caller's name and telephone number, time of call, message or description of the problem, and action taken, if any.				

(continued)

Name ______________________ Class ______________ Date ______________

Procedure Steps Total Possible Points - 24 Time Limit: 10 minutes	Practice #1	Practice #2	Practice #3	Final
5. Repeat the information, confirming that you have the correct spelling of all names.*				
6. When you have retrieved all messages, route them according to the office policy.				
Total Number of Points Achieved/Final Score				
Initials of Observer:				

Comments and Signatures

Reviewer's comments and signatures:

1. ____
2. ____
3. ____

Instructor's comments:

____

Name ______________________ Class ______________ Date __________

CHAPTER 12

Scheduling Appointments and Maintaining the Physician's Schedule

REVIEW

Vocabulary Review

Matching

Match the key terms in the right column with the definitions in the left column by placing the letter of each correct answer in the space provided.

_______ 1. A type of scheduling in which patients arrive at their own convenience, with the understanding that they will be seen on a first-come, first-served basis.

_______ 2. A type of scheduling that works best in large offices that have enough departments and personnel to provide services to several patients at the same time.

_______ 3. A scheduling system in which several patients are given the same appointment time but are taken as they arrive so that the office schedule remains on track each hour even if patients are late.

_______ 4. A type of scheduling in which a patient is booked months ahead of time.

_______ 5. Using double-booking scheduling and clustering scheduling at the same time is an example of this type of technique.

_______ 6. A patient who does not come to his appointment and does not call to cancel it.

_______ 7. A term that describes a patient who has not been established at the medical practice.

_______ 8. A term to describe a patient who is being sent to another physician for a second opinion.

_______ 9. A term used to describe a patient who comes to see the doctor without an appointment.

_______ 10. Another name for stream scheduling.

_______ 11. Leaving large, unused gaps in the schedule.

_______ 12. The appointment book is an example of this type of document.

_______ 13. Contacting a patient to confirm an appointment.

_______ 14. The basic format for an appointment book.

_______ 15. An item that should be discussed with the physician during regularly scheduled meetings.

a. advanced scheduling
b. underbooking
c. matrix
d. referral
e. legal record
f. wave scheduling
g. modified wave scheduling
h. time-specified scheduling
i. no-show
j. walk-in
k. open-hours scheduling
l. new patient
m. combination scheduling
n. tax schedule and payments
o. reminder notice or call

Name ______________________ Class ______________ Date __________

Content Review

Multiple Choice

In the space provided, write the letter of the choice that best completes each statement or answers each question.

_______ 1. A system used typically in emergency centers rather than in private practice is
- A. wave scheduling.
- B. double-booking.
- C. modified-wave scheduling
- D. cluster scheduling.
- E. open-hours scheduling.

_______ 2. What is the purpose of a matrix?
- A. It automatically informs patients of their appointments.
- B. It serves as a basic format for scheduling.
- C. It is used to obtain patient information.
- D. It indicates a referral.
- E. It reminds a medical assistant to call patients to confirm their appointments.

_______ 3. If a patient comes in unexpectedly with an emergency condition, it is vital that
- A. the nearest hospital be notified immediately.
- B. the patient be treated as quickly as the schedule will allow.
- C. a physician see that patient ahead of patients who may already be waiting.
- D. patients who have appointments at that time be given the chance to reschedule.
- E. the patient wait his turn.

_______ 4. A disadvantage of the open-hours scheduling system is that
- A. it assumes that two patients will actually be seen by the doctor within the scheduled period.
- B. it increases the possibility of inefficient down time for the doctor.
- C. patients become annoyed or angry when they realize their appointments are at the same time as other patients.
- D. it always means the patient will have a long wait.

_______ 5. What type of appointment scheduling system can be helpful if a patient calls and needs to be seen that day but no appointments are available?
- A. Stream
- B. Wave
- C. Modified-wave
- D. Cluster
- E. Double-booking

_______ 6. Which appointment scheduling system determines the number of patients to be seen each hour by dividing the hour by the length of the average visit?
- A. Double-booking
- B. Cluster
- C. Wave
- D. Advance
- E. Open-hours

_______ **7.** The appropriate procedure to follow for a patient who misses an appointment is to

A. document the no-show in the appointment book and in the patient's chart.

B. notify the patient that she will be charged for the missed appointment and interest will be applied.

C. refuse to reschedule an appointment for the patient.

D. schedule another appointment for the patient but tell her she must call the day before or the appointment will be canceled.

E. only reschedule the patient with the doctor's approval.

_______ **8.** What should you do when a regular patient comes to the office without an appointment?

A. Ask him how you can help him and notify the physician as needed.

B. Ask him to leave and you will call him later.

C. Take him directly to see the physician.

D. Tell him he can't see the physician without an appointment.

E. Tell him you can't make appointments for walk-ins.

_______ **9.** Obtaining patient information for an appointment should include which of the following?

A. Marital status

B. Religion

C. Age

D. Occupation

E. Purpose of the visit

_______ **10.** If you are asked to take minutes at a medical meeting, you will need to

A. create the agenda for the meeting as well.

B. mail a notice to every person to notify them of the meeting.

C. know how many people are expected at the meeting.

D. prepare a report of what was discussed and decided at the meeting.

E. call everyone and remind them of the date and time of the meeting.

_______ **11.** What does the abbreviation CP stand for?

A. Canceled procedure

B. Complains politely

C. Check progress

D. Chest pain

_______ **12.** Most minor medical problems, such as a sore throat, earache, or blood sugar check, usually require how many minutes?

A. 10 to 15

B. 15 to 20

C. 20 to 30

D. 30 to 45

_______ **13.** The abbreviation Rx stands for?

A. X-ray procedure

B. Treatment

C. Prescription

D. Immunization

_______ **14.** Which of the following is the correct abbreviation for injection?

A. INJ
B. inj
C. I & D
D. INJECT

_______ **15.** Appointments that are anticipated to require more time should be scheduled

A. at the beginning of the hour.
B. at the end of the hour.
C. with another patient's 10-minute time slot.
D. during a 10-minute time slot.

_______ **16.** The appointment book is a legal record and should be kept at least

A. 1 year.
B. 10 years.
C. 5 years.
D. 3 years.

Sentence Completion

In the space provided, write the word or phrase that best completes each sentence.

17. The abbreviation "NP" stands for _______.

18. To save time when entering information in the appointment book, you could use the standard abbreviation CPE to stand for _______.

19. A _______ is a way to remind patients to book an appointment in 6 months.

20. _______ scheduling systems can be programmed to lock out selected appointment slots, which can be saved for emergencies.

21. It is important to document a patient who is a no-show in the appointment book and in the _______.

22. To see a referral on relatively short notice is a matter of _______ to the referring physician.

23. Scheduling more patients than can reasonably be seen in the time allowed is called _______.

24. Appointments are often made outside the medical office for surgeries, consultations with other physicians, and various _______ tests.

25. In general, it is good practice to avoid scheduling diabetic patients for appointments at this time of day: _______.

26. Making travel arrangements for a physician may include securing airline reservations, requesting _______ of room reservations, and picking up tickets.

17. ______________________
18. ______________________
19. ______________________
20. ______________________
21. ______________________
22. ______________________
23. ______________________
24. ______________________
25. ______________________
26. ______________________

Name ______________________ Class ______________ Date __________

Short Answer

Write the answer to each question on the lines provided.

27. Why is it important to not throw away an old appointment book?

28. How can having a list of standard procedures and the time required for each procedure help you be an efficient scheduler?

29. What three pieces of information must you obtain to properly schedule a patient appointment?

30. How does time-specified scheduling work?

31. How would you select a scheduling appointment system for a medical practice?

32. Give three examples of special scheduling situations that would require you to adjust the schedule for patient needs.

33. Which takes more time and why: An established patient visit or a new patient visit?

34. Why is it beneficial to involve the patient in scheduling his outside appointments?

35. When using advanced scheduling, it is still advisable to leave a few appointment slots open each day. Why?

36. What is an agenda?

37. If a physician in your office refers a patient to another doctor, what is your first step?

38. Define locum tenens.

39. What does the abbreviation NS stand for?

40 What does the abbreviation GI stand for?

Critical Thinking

Write the answer to each question on the lines provided.

1. Who is impacted when a patient is late for an appointment?

2. Why might physicians prefer to schedule new patients first thing in the morning?

3. Why is it important to document a no-show in the appointment book and the patient chart?

4. What types of practices may require more than one locum tenens on call to cover during a physician's absence?

5. Why is it important for the medical assistant to stock the physician's bag carefully? What could be the consequences of a medical bag that is not properly stocked?

6. What time of day should fasting patients be scheduled for appointments? Why?

7. If the physician is running behind in the schedule for the day, how might you be able to help?

8. List the information you need to book a patient's appointment.

9. Describe the proper way to document a cancellation or a no-show in the appointment book.

Name ______________________ Class ______________ Date __________

Application

Follow the directions for each application.

1. Scheduling Appointments

Schedule your classmates for appointments at a medical practice.

a. Choose the type of specialty for the practice and the days and hours that the office will be open to see patients each week. Select a scheduling system for your office to use.

b. Determine five procedures (checkups, minor in-office surgeries, and so on) to be performed at the practice. Estimate the typical length of time for each procedure.

c. Schedule the students in your class for appointments, making sure that there is enough time for the procedures to be performed. For each appointment, record the patient's full name, home and work telephone numbers, purpose of visit, and estimated length of visit. Use abbreviations where helpful.

d. Evaluate the schedule for overbooking or underbooking. Share your schedule with another student and ask for comments. Revise the schedule as necessary.

2. Developing a Travel Itinerary

A physician in your practice is attending the American Medical Association's annual conference, to be held at the Hyatt Regency Hotel in Chicago. Develop a travel itinerary that you can give to the physician and also keep a copy of in the office for reference.

a. Determine the dates of the conference and the dates of the physician's departure and return. Choose the airline that the physician will fly and note the flight times.

b. Record the itinerary in chronological order. Include telephone numbers and addresses of each location where the physician can be reached as well as the dates and times that the physician can be reached there.

c. Evaluate your itinerary. Are you able to contact the physician at every point during the trip? If not, is there additional information you can list on the itinerary?

d. Examine itineraries developed by your classmates. Is there something they included in their itineraries that you can add to yours?

e. With your classmates, discuss the value of having an itinerary.

Case Studies

Write your response to each case study on the lines provided.

Case 1

You are new in the office but you feel that the type of scheduling system used in the medical practice is not working well to meet the patient's needs. What could you do?

____

____

____

Case 2

A female patient becomes upset when a man who just arrived at the office is taken to see the doctor immediately. The woman has been waiting for almost an hour and was supposed to be seen next. What should you do?

____

____

____

Name ______________________ Class ______________ Date __________

Case 3

A medical assistant informs waiting patients that the physician will be delayed. She shares details about the emergency appendectomy the mayor's daughter needs, which will take at least an hour. She asks patients whether they prefer to wait, reschedule, or run errands and come back later. Has the medical assistant handled this situation appropriately? Explain.

____

____

____

Case 4

You have been asked to create a cluster schedule for the office. In your own words, describe the steps you would take to set up this new system.

____

____

____

Procedure Competency Checklists

PROCEDURE 12.1 CREATING A CLUSTER SCHEDULE

Procedure Goal

To set up a cluster schedule

Scoring System

To score each step, use the following scoring system:
1 = poor, 2 = fair, 3 = good, 4 = excellent

A minimum score of at least a 3 must be achieved on **each** step to achieve successful completion of the technique. Detailed instructions on the scoring system are found on page x of the Preface.

Materials

Calendar, tickler file, appointment book, colored pencils or markers (optional)

Procedure

Procedure Steps Total Possible Points - 24 Time Limit: 5 minutes	Practice #1	Practice #2	Practice #3	Final
1. Learn which categories of cases the physician would like to cluster and on what days and/or times of day.				
2. Determine the length of the average visit in each category.				
3. In the appointment book, cross out the hours in the week that the physician is typically not available.*				
4. Block out one period in midmorning and one in midafternoon for use as buffer, or reserve, times for unexpected needs.				

(continued)

Name ______________________ Class ______________ Date __________

Procedure Steps Total Possible Points - 24 Time Limit: 5 minutes	Practice #1	Practice #2	Practice #3	Final
5. Reserve additional slots for acutely ill patients. The number of slots depends on the type of practice.*				
6. Mark the appointment times for clustered procedures. If desired, color-code the blocks of time. For example, make immunization clusters pink, blood pressure checks green, and so forth.*				
Total Number of Points Achieved/Final Score				
Initials of Observer:				

Comments and Signatures

Reviewer's comments and signatures:

1. ______________________________

2. ______________________________

3. ______________________________

Instructor's comments:

____

Procedure 12.2 Scheduling and Confirming Surgery at a Hospital

Procedure Goal

To follow the proper procedure for scheduling and confirming surgery

Scoring System

To score each step, use the following scoring system:
1 = poor, 2 = fair, 3 = good, 4 = excellent

A minimum score of at least a 3 must be achieved on **each** step to achieve successful completion of the technique. Detailed instructions on the scoring system are found on page x of the Preface.

Materials

Calendar, telephone, notepad, pen

Procedure

Procedure Steps Total Possible Points - 24 Time Limit: 10 minutes	Practice #1	Practice #2	Practice #3	Final
1. Elective surgery is usually performed on certain days when the doctor is scheduled to be in the operating room and a room and an anesthetist are available. The patient may be given only one or two choices of days and times. (For emergency surgery the first step is to reserve the operating room.)				

(continued)

Name ______________________ Class ______________ Date ____________

Procedure Steps Total Possible Points - 24 Time Limit: 10 minutes	Practice #1	Practice #2	Practice #3	Final
2. Call the operating room secretary. Give the procedure required, the name of the surgeon, the time involved, and the preferred date and hour.				
3. Provide the patient's name (including birth name, if appropriate), address, telephone number, age, gender, Social Security number, and insurance information.*				
4. Call the admissions office (or day-stay surgery office). Arrange for the patient to be admitted on the day of surgery or the day before (depending on the surgery to be performed). Ask for a copy of the admissions form for the patient record.				
5. Some hospitals want patients to complete preadmission forms. In such cases, request a blank form for the patient. Depending on hospital policy, tell the patient to arrive for the appointment a few minutes early to complete the appropriate paperwork.				
6. Confirm the surgery and the patient's arrival time 1 business day before surgery.*				
Total Number of Points Achieved/Final Score				
Initials of Observer:				

Comments and Signatures

Reviewer's comments and signatures:

1. ____

2. ____

3. ____

Instructor's comments:

____

Name ______________________ Class ______________ Date ______________

CHAPTER 13

Patient Reception

REVIEW

Vocabulary Review

True or False

Decide whether each statement is true or false. In the space at the left, write T *for true or* F *for false. On the lines provided, rewrite the false statements to make them true.*

_______ 1. The appearance of the reception area helps to create a patient's impression of the practice.

____

_______ 2. A bandage from a child's cut is infectious waste, but a used diaper is not.

____

_______ 3. The Americans With Disabilities Act protects people against discrimination because of their mental disability.

____

_______ 4. A contagious disease can be spread among patients waiting in a reception area.

____

_______ 5. People from different countries or cultures are considered to be differently abled.

____

_______ 6. A color family is a group of colors that work well together.

____

_______ 7. Examples of specialty items in a reception include chairs and sofas.

____

_______ 8. Patients should have clear, easy access from the parking lot to the medical office door.

____

_______ 9. A TTY is a device for hearing-impaired patients.

____

_______ 10. A bulletin board is appropriate in a medical practice.

____

_______ 11. Health magazines geared toward the general public are a good choice for reading material in a medical office.

____

_______ 12. It is not necessary to read pamphlets and brochures that are displayed in the reception areas as long as they are published by major publishing companies.

____

_______ 13. Some states have a relay service for patients with hearing impairments or those with speech disabilities.

____

_______ 14. No matter how tastefully it is decorated, the reception area will be unappealing if it is not clean.

____

_______ 15. The primary pastime in the patient reception area is watching television.

____

_______ 16. Stuffed animals are appropriate for pediatric reception areas because they are soft.

____

Content Review

Multiple Choice

In the space provided, write the letter of the choice that best answers each question or completes each statement.

_______ 1. The use of videos in a medical practice is

- **A.** always inappropriate.
- **B.** becoming a more common activity.
- **C.** appropriate only for children.
- **D.** appropriate only for adults for teaching purposes.

_______ 2. The best toys for children in a reception area are

- **A.** toys intended for quiet play.
- **B.** toys that can be easily cleaned.
- **C.** toys that can be enjoyed while the child sits.
- **D.** All of the above.
- **E.** None of the above.

_______ 3. A double door leading from the medical office to the outside of the building

- **A.** helps patients feel safe in the waiting area.
- **B.** discourages salespeople from entering.
- **C.** helps patients locate the office.
- **D.** minimizes drafts in the reception area.

_______ 4. Which of the following items would be a good addition to a pediatrician's reception area?

- **A.** Videocassette recorder (VCR) and children's videotapes
- **B.** Sponge ball and bat
- **C.** Stuffed animals
- **D.** Bottle of bubble-blowing liquid
- **E.** Bag of marbles

Name ______________________ Class ______________ Date __________

_______ 5. Items on a reception bulletin board should be
- A. written in very large print.
- B. only related to government reports on food and drugs.
- C. changed daily.
- D. never contain information about drugs.
- E. tailored to patients' interests.

_______ 6. Older patients may require furniture that is
- A. plastic.
- B. firm.
- C. brightly colored.
- D. extra soft to accommodate for their loss of muscle tissue.

_______ 7. The correct amount of furniture in a reception area
- A. is enough furniture so that all patients and family members or friends who accompany the patient can sit comfortably, no matter how busy the office schedule is.
- B. is six chairs and one sofa.
- C. is 10 chairs and no sofas.
- D. depends on the size of the room and the number of windows and is usually six to eight chairs.
- E. is specified by OSHA safety regulations.

_______ 8. The patient information packet includes
- A. magazine articles.
- B. billing and insurance processing policies.
- C. drug information.
- D. medical brochures.

_______ 9. Pediatric reception areas
- A. are designed to meet the special size and needs of children.
- B. are required under federal law for all family practice offices.
- C. are different from traditional reception areas only in that all the furniture is smaller.
- D. are designed only for sick children.
- E. do not differ in any way from adult reception areas.

_______ 10. A cleaning communications notebook is
- A. a means of communication between the office staff and the cleaning staff.
- B. a way to list special cleanup needs for the cleaning staff.
- C. a way to congratulate and thank the cleaning staff.
- D. All of the above.
- E. None of the above.

_______ 11. A telecom teletype machine
- A. is required by federal law in medical practices.
- B. looks just like a regular telephone.
- C. looks like a laptop computer with a cradle for the receiver of a traditional telephone.
- D. is not capable of communicating with another telecom teletype machine.

_______ 12. The Americans With Disabilities Act
- A. specifies that bars or rails are attached exactly 30 inches above the floor.
- B. does not address types of discrimination.
- C. maintains the rights of disabled people, including jobs.
- D. has no impact on the patient reception area of a medical practice.

Name ______________________ Class ______________ Date ____________

Sentence Completion

In the space provided, write the word or phrase that best completes each sentence.

13. Many elderly patients feel colder because of _______. **13.** ______________

14. Music in the reception area should reflect the interests of the _______. **14.** ______________

15. The path patients must take to get from the parking area or street to the office and then back again is called the patient _______. **15.** ______________

16. _______ is waste that can be dangerous to those who handle it or to the environment. **16.** ______________

17. In a large medical office, the cleaning service is often supervised by a(n) _______. **17.** ______________

18. One odor that can be prevented by displaying a sign in a patient reception area is _______. **18.** ______________

19. OSHA requires the regular use of _______ as part of a cleaning schedule. **19.** ______________

20. To protect patients and staff from being trapped by a fire, medical offices are legally required to install _______. **20.** ______________

21. Reading materials in a patient reception area can be organized on tables or in a _______. **21.** ______________

22. To protect all patients, but especially those who are immunocompromised, it is best to take _______ patients directly into the exam room. **22.** ______________

Short Answer

Write the answer to each question on the lines provided.

23. Why are ramps important for a medical practice?

____

____

____

24. What are five daily tasks involved in cleaning a reception area?

____

____

____

25. Why should you take special care in cleaning up after a patient who has vomited or bled on the furniture in the reception area?

____

____

____

26. How much furniture should there be in a patient reception area?

27. How do you best clean a stain?

28. Give two reasons why a medical office should have at least two exits.

29. What are four types of appropriate reading material for the patient reception area?

30. What is the best way to wash artificial flowers?

31. List three ways you could make a reception area more comfortable for elderly patients.

32. List four aspects of a reception area that can make a stay there seem longer than it actually is.

33. How can you best determine the correct temperature for a medical office?

34. List six guidelines for safety in the reception area.

Name ______________________ Class ______________ Date ____________

35. Define office access.

36. List three warm colors.

37. What are three factors to consider in determining the number of parking spaces a medical office needs?

Critical Thinking

Write the answer to each question on the lines provided.

1. Why is it important to keep patients occupied and informed?

2. Describe the best way to calculate how much seating should be in a physician's reception area.

3. What kind of specialty items would you choose to add to the reception area of a geriatric practice?

4. What type of music is best in a medical office and why?

5. Why is it important to clean a patient reception area on a daily basis?

Name ______________________ Class ______________ Date ________

APPLICATION

Follow the directions for the application.

Creating a Reception Area

Working with a partner, imagine that you have been asked to create a patient reception area for a small medical office. As you plan the area, keep the needs and comfort of the patients foremost in your minds.

a. With your partner, decide on the kind of practice for which you will be creating a reception area, such as a gerontology, orthopedic, or family practice. Then brainstorm a list of the characteristics, needs, and interests of the patients of this practice. Put the kind of practice and your list in writing.

b. Determine the size of the reception area. Base the size on the number of patients who will be using the reception area at one time. Make a diagram or floor plan of the area. If you wish, use graph paper and draw the area to scale. For example, you might decide that one square on the graph paper equals 2 feet in the reception area. Locate all doors and windows. Draw them to scale on the diagram.

c. Discuss the decor. Choose a color family, and select colors for the carpeting, furniture, walls, window treatments, and so on. Keep written notes of your selections.

d. Decide what furniture you will purchase and how it will be arranged. Keep in mind the needs of the kinds of patients who will use the reception area. Locate each piece of furniture on your diagram of the area, drawing each to scale.

e. Choose music, specific magazines and books, and special items for the reception area. Write down your choices.

f. Along with other pairs of students, share your diagram and written notes with the class. Join in a class discussion of the various reception area plans and how each area will meet the specific needs of the medical practice and its patients.

CASE STUDIES

Write your response to each case study on the lines provided.

Case 1

The physician is especially fond of tropical fish and wants to add a tropical fish aquarium to the office. You don't know how to correctly care for an aquarium of fish and fear it might be a hazard to young patients. What should you do?

____

____

____

Case 2

One patient visits the medical office where you work at least once a week and brings her two preschoolers. At first, she asked you to keep an eye on them while she was in the exam room. Now she just leaves the children in the reception area, expecting you to babysit without being asked. You cannot stay in the reception area and watch her children. How can you handle this problem?

____

____

____

Name ______________________ Class ______________ Date ____________

Case 3

A pediatric practice has a small paved area just behind the office. Another medical assistant thinks the space could be used for a basketball court where children who are not sick could play while they wait for the doctor to see them or a sibling. Is this a good idea? Explain.

____

____

____

Case 4

You are working in a large medical office along with two other medical assistants. You notice that you are the only one who routinely picks up and cleans the patient reception area. You feel others should be helping maintain this important area. What should you do?

____

____

____

Procedure Competency Checklists

PROCEDURE 13.1 CREATING A PEDIATRIC PLAYROOM

Procedure Goal

To create a play environment for children in the patient reception area of a pediatric practice

Scoring System

To score each step, use the following scoring system:
1 = poor, 2 = fair, 3 = good, 4 = excellent

A minimum score of at least a 3 must be achieved on **each** step to achieve successful completion of the technique. Detailed instructions on the scoring system are found on page x of the Preface.

Materials

Children's books and magazines, games, toys, nontoxic crayons and coloring books, television and videocassette recorder (VCR), children's videotapes, child- and adult-size chairs, child-size table, bookshelf, boxes or shelves, decorative wall hangings or educational posters (optional)

Procedure

Procedure Steps Total Possible Points - 28 Time Limit: 15 minutes	Practice #1	Practice #2	Practice #3	Final
1. Place all adult-size chairs against the wall. Position some of the child-size chairs along the wall with the adult chairs.				
2. Place the remainder of the child-size chairs in small groupings throughout the room. In addition, put several chairs with the child-size table.				
3. Put the books, magazines, crayons, and coloring books on the bookshelf in one corner of the room near a grouping of chairs.				

(continued)

Name ______________________ Class ______________ Date __________

Procedure Steps Total Possible Points - 28 Time Limit: 15 minutes	Practice #1	Practice #2	Practice #3	Final
4. Choose toys and games carefully. Avoid toys that encourage active play, such as balls, or toys that require a large area. Make sure that all toys meet safety guidelines. Watch for loose parts or parts that are smaller than a golf ball. Toys should also be easy to clean.*				
5. Place the activities for older children near one grouping of chairs and the games and toys for younger children near another grouping. Keep the toys and games in a toy box or on shelves designated for them. Consider labeling or color-coding boxes and shelves and the games and toys that belong there to encourage children to return the games and toys to the appropriate storage area.				
6. Place the television and VCR on a high shelf, if possible, or attach it to the wall near the ceiling. Keep children's videos behind the reception desk, and periodically change the video in the VCR.*				
7. To make the room more cheerful, decorate it with wall hangings or posters.				
Total Number of Points Achieved/Final Score				
Initials of Observer:				

Comments and Signatures

Reviewer's comments and signatures:

1. ______________________

2. ______________________

3. ______________________

Instructor's comments:

____

Procedure 13.2 Creating a Reception Area Accessible to Differently Abled Patients

Procedure Goal

To arrange elements in the reception area to accommodate patients who are differently abled

Scoring System

To score each step, use the following scoring system:
1 = poor, 2 = fair, 3 = good, 4 = excellent

A minimum score of at least a 3 must be achieved on **each** step to achieve successful completion of the technique. Detailed instructions on the scoring system are found on page x of the Preface.

Materials

Ramps (if needed), doorway floor coverings, chairs, bars or rails, adjustable-height tables, magazine rack, television/VCR or DVD player, large-type and Braille magazines

Name ______________________ Class ______________ Date ____________

Procedure

Procedure Steps Total Possible Points - 40 Time Limit: 15 minutes	Practice #1	Practice #2	Practice #3	Final
1. Arrange chairs, leaving gaps so that substantial space is available for wheelchairs along walls and near other groups of chairs. Keep the arrangement flexible so that chairs can be removed to allow room for additional wheelchairs if needed.*				
2. Remove any obstacles that may interfere with the space needed for a wheelchair to swivel around completely. Also remove scatter rugs or any carpeting that is not attached to the floor. Such carpeting can cause patients to trip and create difficulties for wheelchair traffic.*				
3. Position coffee tables at a height that is accessible to people in wheelchairs.				
4. Place office reading materials, such as magazines, at a height that is accessible to people in wheelchairs (for example, on tables or in racks attached midway up the wall).				
5. Locate the television and VCR within full view of patients sitting on chairs and in wheelchairs so that they do not have to strain their necks to watch.				
6. For patients who have a vision impairment, include reading materials with large type and in Braille.				
7. For patients who have difficulty walking, make sure bars or rails are attached securely to walls 34 to 38 inches above the floor, to accommodate requirements set forth in the Americans With Disabilities Act. Make sure the bars are sturdy enough to provide balance for patients who may need it. Bars are most important in entrances and hallways, as well as in the bathroom. Consider placing a bar near the receptionist's window for added support as patients check in.*				
8. Eliminate sills of metal or wood along the floor in doorways. Otherwise, create a smoother travel surface for wheelchairs and pedestrians with a thin rubber covering to provide a graduated slope. Be sure that the covering is attached properly and meets safety standards.*				
9. Make sure the office has ramp access.*				
10. Solicit feedback from patients with physical disabilities about the accessibility of the patient reception area. Encourage ideas for improvements. Address any additional needs.*				
Total Number of Points Achieved/Final Score				
Initials of Observer:				

Comments and Signatures

Reviewer's comments and signatures:

1. ______________________________

2. ______________________________

3. ______________________________

Instructor's comments:

____

Name ______________________ Class ______________ Date __________

CHAPTER 14

Patient Education

Review

Vocabulary Review

Passage Completion

Study the key terms in the box. Use your textbook to find definitions of terms you do not understand.

consumer education	modeling	return demonstration	screening

In the space provided, complete the following passage, using the terms from the box. You may change the form of a term to fit the meaning of the sentence.

Patient education is a vital part of patient care. Preoperative teaching, for example, increases patients' knowledge about and participation in the surgical procedure. Through factual teaching and active demonstrations that include (1) _______, patients learn techniques that can enhance their recovery. The patient should repeat any demonstration, a practice that is called (2) _______. (3) _______ that is geared to the average person, in content and in language, helps increase awareness of the importance of good health. This kind of education includes encouraging patients to have regular (4) _______ tests for early diagnosis and treatment of certain diseases. Patients also benefit from learning about the medical office.

1. ______________________
2. ______________________
3. ______________________
4. ______________________

Content Review

Multiple Choice

In the space provided, write the letter of the choice that best completes each statement or answers each question.

_______ 1. Which of the following terms is used to describe an office's set of values and principles?

A. Screening technique
B. Benefits
C. Confidentiality
D. Philosophy
E. Privacy rules

_______ **2.** Which of the following topics would an educational newsletter most likely contain?

A. Health-care tips
B. A physician's credentials
C. The payment policies of a medical office
D. A community resource directory
E. A list of the office's staff

_______ **3.** The process of screening

A. doesn't allow an early diagnosis.
B. is free.
C. differs according to patient age.
D. is only advisable when symptoms are present.
E. can't be done in a medical practice.

_______ **4.** Some practices create simplified versions of their patient information packet for patients

A. with hearing impairments.
B. with visual impairments.
C. who do not understand English.
D. who will undergo surgical procedures.

_______ **5.** When speaking to a patient who wears a hearing aid, it is best to

A. filter out loud noises.
B. raise your voice.
C. speak at a normal level.
D. speak very slowly.
E. write down everything.

_______ **6.** It is recommended that the water in the water heater be set at what temperature in order to prevent injury?

A. 100°F
B. 120°F
C. 130°F
D. 140°F

_______ **7.** When developing a patient education plan, the first thing you must do is

A. develop the plan.
B. discuss the idea with the physician.
C. perform the instruction.
D. identify how intelligent the patient is.
E. identify the patient's needs.

_______ **8.** Which of these is the best definition of patient education?

A. Patient education is the use of visual material to educate a patient.
B. Patient education is the demonstration of a technique to a patient.
C. Patient education is the use of verbal instruction to educate a patient.
D. Any instructions—verbal, written, or demonstrative—that are given to patients are types of patient education.

_______ **9.** Which statement about patient education is true?

A. Patient education is always performed according to a well-defined plan.
B. Patient education is only appropriate for intelligent people.
C. Patient education takes many forms and includes a variety of techniques.
D. Medical assistants are not generally involved in patient education.
E. The physician is responsible for providing all patient education.

_______ **10.** Many accidents happen because people fail to see potential risks. *Potential risks* means

A. side effects.
B. situations or things that can cause harm.
C. preventive measures.
D. situations or things that always cause harm.

_______ **11.** *Preventive measures* means

A. patient education.
B. health-promoting behaviors.
C. screening.
D. anything that helps a patient avoid illness or injury.

_______ **12.** The patient information packet should include

A. the first bill or invoice.
B. names of other medical practices that the practice is not associated with.
C. medical brochures describing disease processes that relate to the patient's primary medical condition.
D. a description of the practice and an introduction to the office.
E. referrals to other physicians.

_______ **13.** The patient confidentiality statement

A. supplies a place for the patient to sign before any other practice information is released.
B. is not commonly used in a pediatric practice.
C. should state that no information from patient files will be released without signed authorization from the patient.
D. is not usually part of the information packet.

_______ **14.** The guidelines for healthful habits include adequate rest, which is defined as being how many hours of sleep each night?

A. 7 to 8
B. 8 to 9
C. 5 to 6
D. 10 or more hours

Sentence Completion

In the space provided, write the word or phrase that best completes each sentence.

15. Many accidents happen because people fail to see _______ and do not develop plans of action.

16. Health is a complex concept that involves the body, _______, emotions, and environment.

17. The first letter of the warning signs for cancer spell out the word _______.

15. ______________________

16. ______________________

17. ______________________

18. A patient information packet should identify office staff members according to their _______.

19. Elderly patients who have problems with memory should receive detailed _______ instructions.

20. Patients who will undergo a surgical procedure must first sign a(n) _______ form.

21. When you provide preoperative education, be aware that the fear and _______ of patients who are about to undergo a surgical procedure can adversely affect the learning process.

18. ______________________

19. ______________________

20. ______________________

21. ______________________

Short Answer

Write the answer to each question on the lines provided.

22. Why is patient education so important prior to surgery?

23. List three ways to achieve good health.

24. What is the general function of an occupational therapy assistant?

25. What are three ways that a patient information packet can be helpful to patients? To a medical office?

26. List five types of information that should appear in a patient information packet.

27. When providing information to elderly patients, what are some important points to remember?

Name ______________________________ Class ________________ Date __________

28. Name some materials that are available for patient education in the public library.

____

____

____

29. Identify and describe three types of preoperative teaching.

____

____

____

30. Of the healthy habits listed in this chapter, which three do you consider the most important and why?

____

____

____

31. List six practices that a medical assistant should use when educating patients with hearing problems.

____

____

____

32. List three ways you can relieve a patient's anxiety.

____

____

____

33. List five tips for preventing injury in the workplace.

____

____

____

34. How might you explain to a patient the proper use of medications?

____

____

____

35. List the eight steps to developing an education plan for a patient.

____

____

____

36. Why is it important for a surgical patient to have someone drive her home after surgery?

____

____

____

Name ______ Class ______ Date ______

Critical Thinking

Write the answer to each question on the lines provided.

1. What are the advantages of developing a formal, written educational plan for a patient?

2. How might your approach to educating children about healthful habits differ from your approach to teaching adult patients?

3. What type of preoperative teaching plan do you think might be best for a patient who is blind?

4. When educating patients with special needs, why is it important to be especially sensitive to their individual circumstances?

5. What do you think is the most important tip for preventing injury in the workplace? Why?

APPLICATION

Follow the directions for the application.

Preparing a Patient Information Packet

Work with a partner to write the following portions of a patient information packet for a fictional medical practice: introduction to the office, description of the practice, introduction to the office staff, office hours, procedures for scheduling and canceling appointments, telephone policy, payment policies, insurance policies, and patient confidentiality statement.

a. Decide on the type of practice to write about. Determine the size of the practice and the number of physicians and other staff members.

b. Reread the description of the contents of a patient information packet. Keep in mind that material in the packet must be written in a clear, straightforward style. Make notes on types of information that will appear in each section of the packet.

c. Decide whether your packet will be a one- or two-page brochure or pamphlet, a multipage booklet, or a folder with several inserts.

d. Determine the order in which information will appear in the packet.

e. On notebook paper, write specific information for each topic.

f. Review and revise the information to ensure that it is clear and complete.

g. Prepare a mock-up of your patient information packet, using sheets of drawing paper and a folder, if you are using one.

h. Copy the information under appropriate headings in the mock-up of your packet. Add illustrations, diagrams, or a map, where appropriate.

i. Share your patient information packet with other pairs in the class. Discuss differences in the packets and point out elements that are particularly effective or helpful for patients.

j. Help prepare a classroom display of the packets. Invite everyone in the class to view and read the packets.

k. In a full-class discussion, describe the most important points for medical assistants to keep in mind when preparing a patient information packet. Suggest ways to distribute packets to patients.

Case Studies

Write your response to each case study on the lines provided.

Case 1

During a physical exam, a teenage patient admits to you that he lives "mainly on hamburgers and French fries," that he rarely exercises, and that he often gets fewer than 6 hours of sleep a night, except on weekends. "I'll worry about my health when I'm older," he tells you. What can you say to the patient to encourage him to adopt healthful habits now?

____

____

____

Case 2

The physician you work for wants you to develop patient information that will fit on two sides of a 4- by 6-inch index card. There will be room for only the most important information. What should appear on the card?

____

____

____

Case 3

The third level of disease prevention involves the rehabilitation and management of an existing illness. What might you say to a patient who thinks that rehabilitation is just a waste of time and money?

____

____

____

Case 4

A patient calls with questions about her upcoming surgery. Her patient record reflects that the physician has already discussed the nature of the surgery with her. As a medical assistant, what are your responsibilities for ensuring that the patient is fully prepared for the surgery?

____

____

____

Name ______________________ Class ______________ Date ____________

Procedure Competency Checklists

PROCEDURE 14.1 DEVELOPING A PATIENT EDUCATION PLAN

Procedure Goal

To create and implement a patient teaching plan

Scoring System

To score each step, use the following scoring system:
1 = poor, 2 = fair, 3 = good, 4 = excellent

A minimum score of at least a 3 must be achieved on **each** step to achieve successful completion of the technique. Detailed instructions on the scoring system are found on page x of the Preface.

Materials

Pen, paper, various educational aids such as instructional pamphlets and brochures, and/or visual aids such as posters, videotapes, or DVDs

Procedure

Procedure Steps Total Possible Points - 32 Time Limit: 15 minutes	Practice #1	Practice #2	Practice #3	Final
1. Identify the patient's educational needs. Consider the following: a. The patient's current knowledge b. Any misconceptions the patient may have c. Any obstacles to learning (loss of hearing or vision, limitations of mobility, language barriers, and so on) d. The patient's willingness and readiness to learn (motivation) e. How the patient will use the information*				
2. Develop and outline a plan using the various educational aids available. Include the following areas in the outline: a. What you want to accomplish (your goal) b. How you plan to accomplish it c. How you will determine if the teaching was successful*				
3. Write the plan. Try to make the information interesting for the patient.				
4. Before carrying out the plan, share it with the physician to get approval and suggestions for improvement.				
5. Perform the instruction. Be sure to use more than one teaching method. For instance, if written material is being given, be sure to explain or demonstrate the material instead of simply telling the patient to read the educational materials.				
6. Document the teaching in the patient's chart.*				

(continued)

Name ______________________ Class ______________ Date ____________

Procedure Steps Total Possible Points - 32 Time Limit: 15 minutes	Practice #1	Practice #2	Practice #3	Final
7. Evaluate the effectiveness of your teaching session. Ask yourself: a. Did you cover all the topics in your plan? b. Was the information well received by the patient? c. Did the patient appear to learn? d. How would you rate your performance?				
8. Revise your plan as necessary to make it even more effective.*				
Total Number of Points Achieved/Final Score				
Initials of Observer:				

Comments and Signatures

Reviewer's comments and signatures:

1. ______________________________

2. ______________________________

3. ______________________________

Instructor's comments:

____

Procedure 14.2 Informing the Patient of Guidelines for Surgery

Procedure Goal

To inform a preoperative patient of the necessary guidelines to follow prior to surgery

Scoring System

To score each step, use the following scoring system:
1 = poor, 2 = fair, 3 = good, 4 = excellent

A minimum score of at least a 3 must be achieved on **each** step to achieve successful completion of the technique. Detailed instructions on the scoring system are found on page x of the Preface.

Materials

Patient chart, surgical guidelines

Procedure

Procedure Steps Total Possible Points - 56 Time Limit: 10 minutes	Practice #1	Practice #2	Practice #3	Final
1. Review the patient's chart to determine the type of surgery to be performed and then ask the patient what procedure is being performed.*				
2. Tell the patient that you will be providing both verbal and written instructions that should be followed prior to surgery.				

(continued)

Name ______________________ Class ______________ Date ________

Procedure Steps Total Possible Points - 56 Time Limit: 10 minutes	Practice #1	Practice #2	Practice #3	Final
3. Inform the patient about policies regarding makeup, jewelry, contact lenses, wigs, dentures, and so on.				
4. Tell the patient to leave money and valuables at home.				
5. If applicable, suggest appropriate clothing for the patient to wear for postoperative ease and comfort.				
6. Explain the need for someone to drive the patient home following an outpatient surgical procedure.*				
7. Tell the patient the correct time to arrive in the office or at the hospital for the procedure.				
8. Inform the patient of dietary restrictions. Be sure to use specific, clear instructions about what may or may not be ingested and at what time the patient must abstain from eating or drinking. Also explain these points: a. The reasons for the dietary restrictions. b. The possible consequences of not following the dietary restrictions.*				
9. Ask patients who smoke to refrain from or reduce cigarette smoking during at least the 8 hours prior to the procedure. Explain to the patient that reducing smoking improves the level of oxygen in the blood during surgery.				
10. Suggest that the patient shower or bathe the morning of the procedure or the evening before.				
11. Instruct the patient about medications to take or avoid before surgery.*				
12. If necessary, clarify any information about which the patient is unclear.				
13. Provide written surgical guidelines and suggest that the patient call the office if additional questions arise.*				
14. Document the instruction in the patient's chart.*				
Total Number of Points Achieved/Final Score				
Initials of Observer:				

Comments and Signatures

Reviewer's comments and signatures:

1. ______________________________

2. ______________________________

3. ______________________________

Instructor's comments:

____

Name ______________________ Class ______________ Date __________

CHAPTER 15

Health Insurance Billing Procedures

REVIEW

Vocabulary Review

Matching

Match the key terms in the right column with the definitions in the left column by placing the letter of each correct answer in the space provided.

_______ **1.** A health benefit program designed for low-income, blind, or disabled patients; needy families; foster children; and children born with birth defects

_______ **2.** Payments made by an insurance carrier to a policyholder

_______ **3.** A fixed dollar amount that must be paid or "met" once a year before the third-party payer begins to cover medical expenses

_______ **4.** The basic annual cost of health-care insurance paid by a policyholder

_______ **5.** An organization the patient has a relationship with that agrees to carry the risk of paying for medical services

_______ **6.** Authorization from a physician for a patient to receive additional services from another physician or medical facility

_______ **7.** The oldest and most expensive type of health plan, it repays policyholders for costs of health-care due to illness and accidents

_______ **8.** A health-care benefit system for families of veterans with total, permanent, service-connected disabilities and for surviving spouses and children of veterans who died in the line of duty

_______ **9.** A type of insurance, either provided by an employer for its employees or purchased privately by self-employed individuals, that is activated when the employee is injured.

_______ **10.** An outside service that processes and transmits claims in the correct EDI format

_______ **11.** The manager of the Medicare program

_______ **12.** A form that accompanies payment by an insurer and that can include information about services not covered

_______ **13.** The payment system used by Medicare

_______ **14.** The PCP physician payment structure used by most HMOs

_______ **15.** A plan that reimburses the patient's Part B deductible and coinsurance amounts after Medicare pays its portion

_______ **16.** An effort by insurers to prevent duplication of payment for health care

a. deductible
b. capitation
c. CMS
d. CHAMPVA
e. third-party payer
f. coordination of benefits
g. remittance advice (RA)
h. fee-for-service
i. clearinghouse
j. Medigap
k. Medicaid
l. premium
m. disability insurance
n. referral
o. benefits
p. resource-based relative value scale

Name ________________________ Class ______________ Date ____________

True or False

Decide whether each statement is true or false. In the space at the left, write T *for true or* F *for false. On the lines provided, rewrite the false statements to make them true.*

_______ **17.** CHAMPVA covers the expenses of the dependents of veterans with total, permanent, service-connected disabilities.

____

_______ **18.** Some insurers require subscribers to pay a yearly deductible before charges are considered for payment.

____

_______ **19.** TRICARE is a Medicaid program.

____

_______ **20.** A managed care organization (MCO) sets up agreements with physicians as well as with enrolled policyholders.

____

_______ **21.** If a retired patient is covered by the plan of the spouse's employer and the spouse is still employed, Medicare coverage is primary.

____

_______ **22.** Exclusions are expenses covered by an insurance company.

____

_______ **23.** Medicare states that for services rendered from January 1 to September 30, claims must be filed by December 31 of the following year.

____

_______ **24.** Copayments are made to insurance companies.

____

_______ **25.** If an insurance carrier reviews a claim and determines that the diagnosis and the accompanying treatment plan are not compatible, the insurance carrier will not pay for the services rendered.

____

_______ **26.** The RBRVS system is the basis for the Medicare payment system.

____

_______ **27.** The procedure code gives the insurance carrier information regarding medical necessity.

____

_______ **28.** Preferred provider organizations (PPOs) never allow their members to receive care from providers outside the network.

____

_______ **29.** Simple errors often prevent the generation of a "clean" claim.

____

_______ **30.** A lifetime maximum benefit is established as a total dollar amount to be paid by an insurer.

____

_______ **31.** When completing a CMS-1500 claim form for a TRICARE patient, section #4 should always be completed with the name of the patient.

____

_______ **32.** Recipients of Medicare Part A and Part B can purchase Medigap insurance to cover gaps in health insurance coverage.

____

_______ **33.** A taxonomy code is a 10-digit number that stands for a physician's medical specialty.

____

Content Review

Multiple Choice

In the space provided, write the letter of the choice that best completes each statement or answers each question.

_______ **1.** Which of the following is a Medicare plan that charges a monthly premium and a small copayment for each office visit, but no deductible?

A. Medicare managed care plan
B. Medicare preferred provider organization plan
C. Medicare private fee-for-service plan
D. Original Medicare plan
E. Medigap plan

_______ **2.** At the time of service, if required by the managed care plan, medical assistants collect

A. deductibles.
B. copayments.
C. premiums.
D. coinsurance.

_______ **3.** The nationally uniform relative value of a procedure is based on which of the following three things?

A. The physician's specialty, the cost of living, and insurance rates
B. The age of the patient, the diagnosis of the patient, and the geographic area of the practice
C. The amount billed by the physician, the cost of the procedure, and the copayment of the patient
D. The physician's work, the practice's overhead, and the cost of malpractice insurance
E. The fee schedule of the physician, the geographic area of the practice, and the diagnosis of the patient

_______ **4.** Under the concept of the resource-based relative value scale (RBRVS) used by Medicare, the fee for a procedure is based on

A. a formula based on using the relative value, the geographic adjustment factor, and a conversion factor.
B. the generally accepted fee that a physician charges for difficult or complicated services.
C. the average fee that a physician charges for a service or procedure.
D. the 90th percentile of fees charged for a procedure by similar physicians in the same area.

_______ **5.** Billing a patient for the difference between a higher usual fee and a lower allowed charge is called _______ and is not allowed by participating physicians.

A. capitation
B. assignment of benefits
C. coordination of benefits
D. third-party paying
E. balance billing

_______ **6.** Under Medicare Part B, patients are required to pay an annual

A. deductible.
B. copayment.
C. coinsurance.
D. claim submission charge for reimbursement.

_______ **7.** Medicare Part A does not pay for

A. inpatient expenses up to 90 days for each benefit period.
B. medical care at home.
C. outpatient hospital services.
D. psychiatric hospitalization.
E. respite care.

_______ **8.** Patients enrolled in the Original Medicare Plan may purchase additional coverage under a

A. Medicare Part A plan.
B. coinsurance plan.
C. Medigap plan.
D. Medicare Advantage plan.
E. fee-for-service.

Sentence Completion

In the space provided, write the word or phrase that best completes each sentence.

9. The largest federal health-care program is ____________.

10. An insured's policy can also cover _______ of the subscriber, such as a spouse and children.

11. By law, physicians who participate in federally funded programs such as Medicare must accept the _______ charge as payment in full.

12. Patients sign a(n) _______ of benefits statement to permit providers to receive payments directly from third-party payers.

13. Physicians who enroll in managed care plans are called ______________________________.

14. When filing a Medicaid claim, you should ask for and check the patient's Medicaid card to confirm the patient's _______.

15. Managed care plans pay physicians in one of two ways: by either contracted fees or a fixed prepayment called ____________.

9. ______________________________
10. ______________________________
11. ______________________________
12. ______________________________
13. ______________________________
14. ______________________________
15. ______________________________

Name ______________________ Class ______________ Date __________

Short Answer

Write the answer to each question on the lines provided.

16. List three of the basic steps in the claims process that are performed in a doctor's office.

17. What does an eligible individual have to do to receive Medicare Part B?

18. Describe the process used to calculate what the practice must write off and what a patient owes when the provider is a Medicare participating physician.

19. What does liability insurance cover?

20. Why must the X12 837 Health Care Claim be used for Medicare claims?

21. Describe a PPO. How does it operate?

22. List the five sections of data elements on the X12 837 Health Care Claim.

23. What is the purpose of the coordination of benefits clauses in insurance policies?

Name ______________________ Class ______________ Date ________

Critical Thinking

Write the answer to each question on the lines provided.

1. What could be the possible outcome of inaccurate medical billing?

2. For a medical practice, what are some advantages and disadvantages of filing claims for patients rather than having patients pay their medical expenses and file their own claims?

3. Why is it important to follow all claims security procedures when electronically submitting health claims?

4. Technology known as the "smart card" has been developed to store a person's complete medical history. The information would be easy to access, update, and transmit. Do you foresee any problems with such a system?

5. What aspect of a claim do you think is the most difficult to complete and why? How might you get help to complete this part?

Application

Follow the directions for the application.

Developing Tools for Processing Claims

Work with a partner to analyze the information needed to calculate the practice and patient payments for a new medical practice. The practice will accept patients who have Medicare, Medicaid, workers' compensation insurance, managed care plans, and other types of insurance. The practice will use electronic claims processing.

a. Begin by working with your partner to compile a list of items required for the claims processing steps in your medical office. Include the names of forms (such as the patient registration form); carrier rules (such as time limits); logs; and documents. If you cannot recall the exact name of a publication or form, write a brief description of the information it contains.

b. Review sections of Chapter 15 that describe claims processing for various health plans, such as Medicare, Medicaid, TRICARE and CHAMPVA, Blue Cross and Blue Shield, and PPOs. Add items to the list you began in step **a,** such as each plan's premium, deductible, coinsurance, and copayment.

c. Write a brief explanation of how each item is used in processing claims.

d. Identify and list sources of the items, if this information is given in the chapter. If possible, research websites for the information using a Web browser.

e. Organize the list by category of items or by type of insurance coverage or benefit on a chart or other type of graphic organizer.

f. Share your chart with other pairs in the class. Discuss various ways to organize these materials in a medical office.

g. In a full-class discussion, analyze the medical assistant's role in handling health-care claims in terms of the procedures and tools needed to comply with current requirements. Discuss ways to reduce the amount of paperwork involved in filing claims. Offer creative suggestions for streamlining or eliminating some steps in the process.

Case Studies

Write your response to each case study on the lines provided.

Case 1

A new patient is completing your office's patient registration form. The patient tells you that she has insurance but does not have her card with her and does not know the effective date of coverage, the group plan number, or the identification number. Explain one or more ways to obtain the insurance information right away.

____

____

____

Case 2

Your medical office receives a payment and a remittance advice (RA) from an insurer in response to a claim you filed for a patient. The RA notes that one of the services on the claim is not covered in the patient's plan. What steps will you take regarding the rejected portion of the claim?

____

____

____

Case 3

A medical assistant coworker tells you that he doesn't see the point for all the security policies involved with submitting electronic claims. "After all," he says, "all the security we need is built into the system." How might you respond?

____

____

____

Name ____________________ Class ____________ Date ________

Procedure Competency Checklists

PROCEDURE 15.1 VERIFYING WORKERS' COMPENSATION COVERAGE

Procedure Goal

To verify workers' compensation coverage before accepting a patient

Scoring System

To score each step, use the following scoring system:
1 = poor, 2 = fair, 3 = good, 4 = excellent

A minimum score of at least a 3 must be achieved on **each** step to achieve successful completion of the technique. Detailed instructions on the scoring system are found on page x of the Preface.

Materials

Telephone, paper, pencil

Procedure

Procedure Steps Total Possible Points - 24 Time Limit: 10 minutes	Practice #1	Practice #2	Practice #3	Final
1. Call the patient's employer and verify that the accident or illness occurred on the employer's premises or at an employment-related work site.				
2. Obtain the employer's approval to provide treatment. Be sure to write down the name and title of the person giving approval, as well as his phone number.*				
3. Ask the employer for the name of its workers' compensation insurance company. (Employers are required by law to carry such insurance. It is a good policy to notify your state labor department about any employer you encounter that does not have workers' compensation insurance, although you are not required to do so.) You may wish to remind the employer to report any workplace accidents or injuries that result in a workers' compensation claim to the state labor department within 24 hours of the incident.*				
4. Contact the insurance company and verify that the employer does indeed have a policy with the company and that the policy is in good standing.*				
5. Obtain a claim number for the case from the insurance company. This claim number is used on all bills and paperwork.*				

(continued)

Name ______________________ Class ______________ Date ________

Procedure Steps Total Possible Points - 24 Time Limit: 10 minutes	Practice #1	Practice #2	Practice #3	Final
6. At the time the patient starts treatment, create a patient record. If the patient is already one of the practice's regular patients, create separate medical and financial records for the workers' compensation case.*				
Total Number of Points Achieved/Final Score				
Initials of Observer:				

Comments and Signatures

Reviewer's comments and signatures:

1. ______________________

2. ______________________

3. ______________________

Instructor's comments:

____

Procedure 15.2 Completing the CMS-1500 Claim Form

Procedure Goal

To complete the CMS-1500 claim form correctly

Scoring System

To score each step, use the following scoring system:
1 = poor, 2 = fair, 3 = good, 4 = excellent

A minimum score of at least a 3 must be achieved on **each** step to achieve successful completion of the technique. Detailed instructions on the scoring system are found on page x of the Preface.

Materials

Patient record, CMS-1500 form, typewriter or computer, patient ledger card or charge slip

Procedure

Procedure Steps Total Possible Points - 132 Time Limit: 30 minutes	Practice #1	Practice #2	Practice #3	Final
Note: The numbers below correspond to the numbered fields on the CMS-1500.				
Patient Information Section				
1. Place an *X* in the appropriate insurance box.*				
1a. Enter the insured's insurance identification number as it appears on the insurance card.*				

(continued)

Name ______________________ Class ______________ Date __________

Procedure Steps Total Possible Points - 132 Time Limit: 30 minutes	Practice #1	Practice #2	Practice #3	Final
2. Enter the patient's name in this order: last name, first name, middle initial (if any).				
3. Enter the patient's birth date using two digits each for the month and day. For example, for a patient born on February 9, 1954, enter 02-09-1954. Indicate the sex of the patient: male or female.				
4. If the insured and the patient are the same person, enter SAME. If not, enter the policyholder's name. For TRICARE claims, enter the sponsor's (service person's) full name. For Medicare, leave blank.				
5. Enter the patient's mailing address, city, state, and zip code.				
6. Enter the patient's relationship to the insured. If they are the same, mark SELF. For TRICARE, enter the patient's relationship to the sponsor. For Medicare, leave blank.				
7. Enter the insured's mailing address, city, state, zip code, and telephone number. If this address is the same as the patient's, enter SAME. For Medicare, leave blank.				
8. Indicate the patient's marital, employment, and student status by placing an *X* in the boxes.				
9. Enter the last name, first name, and middle initial of any other insured person whose policy might cover the patient. If the claim is for Medicare and the patient has a Medigap policy, enter the patient's name again. Keep in mind that block 9 is for secondary insurance coverage; block 11 is for the patient's primary insurance plan. 9a. Enter the policy or group number for the other insured person. If this is a Medigap policy, enter MEDIGAP before the policy number. For Medicare, leave blank. 9b. Enter the date of birth and sex of the other insured person (field 9). 9c. Enter the other insured's employer or school name. (Note: If this is a Medicare claim, enter the claims-processing address for the Medigap insurer from field 9. If this is a Medicaid claim and other insurance is available, note it in field 1a and in field 2, and enter the requested policy information. 9d. Enter the other insured's insurance plan or program name. If the plan is Medigap and CMS has assigned it a nine-digit number called PAYERID, enter that number here. On an attached sheet, give the complete mailing address for all other insurance information, and enter the word ATTACHMENT in 10d.				
10. Place *X*s in the appropriate YES or NO boxes in a, b, and c to indicate whether the patient's place of employment, an auto accident, or other type of accident precipitated the patient's condition. If an auto accident is responsible, for PLACE, enter the two-letter state postal abbreviation. For Medicaid claims, enter MCD and the Medicaid number at line 10d. If an auto accient is responsible all other claims, enter ATTACHMENT here if there is other insurance information. Be sure the full names and addresses of the other insurers appear on the attached sheet. Also, code the insurer as follows: MSP Medicare Secondary Payer, MG Medigap, SP Supplemental Employer, MCD Medicaid.*				

(continued)

Name ______________________ Class ______________ Date __________

Procedure Steps Total Possible Points - 132 Time Limit: 30 minutes	Practice #1	Practice #2	Practice #3	Final
11. Enter the insured's policy or group number. For Medicare claims, fill out this section only if there is other insurance primary to Medicare; otherwise, enter NONE and leave fields 11a–d blank.* 11a. Enter the insured's date of birth and sex as in field 3, if the insured is not the patient. 11b. Enter the employer's name or school name here. This information will determine if Medicare is the primary payer. 11c. Enter the insurance plan or program name. 11d. Place an *X* to indicate YES or NO related to another health benefit plan. If YES, you must complete 9a through 9d. Failure to do so will cause the claim to be denied. *Note:* It is important to remember that section 11 is for the primary insurer and section 9 is for any secondary insurance coverage.				
12. Have the patient or an authorized representative sign and date the form here. If a representative signs, have the representative indicate the relationship to the patient. If a signature is kept on file in the office, indicate by inserting "signature on file."*				
13. Have the insured (the patient or another individual) sign here.*				
Physician Information Section				
14. Enter the date of the current illness, injury, or pregnancy, using eight digits.				
15. *Do not complete this field.* Leave it blank for Medicare.				
16. Enter the dates the patient is or was unable to work. This information could signal a workers' compensation claim.				
17. Enter the name of the referring physician, clinical laboratory, or other referring source. 17a. If the provider does not have an NPI, enter the appropriate two digit qualifier in the small space immediately to the right of 17a. Next to this, enter the appropriate provider identifier. 17b. If the provider has an NPI number, enter it here.*				
18. Enter the dates the patient was hospitalized, if at all, with the current condition.				
19. Use your payer's current instructions for this field. Some payers require you to enter the date the patient was last seen by the referring physician or other medical professional. Other payers ask for certain identifiers. If an NPI is not available, be sure to use the appropriate non-NPI qualifier to identify the identifier used.				
20. Place an *X* in the YES box if a laboratory test was performed outside the physician's office, and enter the test price if you are billing for these tests. Ensure that field 32 carries the laboratory's exact name and address and the insurance carrier's nine-digit provider identification number (PIN). Place an *X* in the NO box if the test was done in the office of the physician who is billing the insurance company.				

(continued)

Name ______________________________ Class ____________________ Date ____________

Procedure Steps Total Possible Points - 132 Time Limit: 30 minutes	Practice #1	Practice #2	Practice #3	Final
21. Enter the multidigit *International Classification of Diseases, 9th edition, Clinical Modification* (ICD-9-CM) code number diagnosis or nature of injury (see Chapter 16). Enter up to four codes in order of importance. *Note:* Some insurers are allowing up 6 or 8 diagnoses, particularly on electronic claims. Be sure to check with each carrier for its regulations.*				
22. Enter the Medicaid resubmission code and original reference number if applicable.				
23. Enter the prior authorization number if required by the payer.*				
24. The 6 service lines in block 24 are divided horizontally to accommodate NPI and other proprietary identifiers. The upper shaded area may also be used to provide supplemental information regarding services provided, but you must verify requirements for the use of this area with each payer prior to use. Otherwise, use the nonshaded areas. 24A. Enter the date of each service, procedure, or supply provided. Add the number of days for each, and enter them, in chronological order, in field 24G. 24B. Enter the two-digit place-of-service code. For example, 11 is for office, 12 is for home, and 25 is for birthing center. Your office should have a list for reference. 24C. EMC stands for *emergency care.* Check with provider to see if this information is needed. If it is required and emergency care was provided, enter *Y*; if it is not required or care was not on an emergency basis, leave this field blank. For medicare, leave blank. 24D. Enter the CPT/HCPCS codes with modifiers for the procedures, services, or supplies provided (see Chapter 16). 24E. Enter the diagnosis code (or its reference number—1, 2, 3, or 4—depending on carrier regulations) that applies to that procedure, as listed in field 21.* 24F. Enter the dollar amount of fee charged. 24G. Enter the days or units on which the service was performed. If a service took 3 days or was performed 3 times, as listed in 24A, enter 3. 24H. This field is Medicaid-specific for early periodic screening, diagnosis and treatment programs. 24I. If the provider does not have an NPI, enter the appropriate qualifier, indicating the identification number being used in the shaded area. If an NPI is being used, leave this area blank. 24J. If a non-NPI number is being used, enter the insurance-company-assigned nine-digit physician PIN in the shaded area. If an NPI is available, use the NPI number, placing it in the nonshaded area next to the premarked NPI in field 24I.				
25. Enter the physician's or care provider's federal tax identification number or Social Security number.				
26. Enter the patient's account number assigned by your office, if applicable.				

(continued)

Name ______________________________ Class ____________________ Date ____________

Procedure Steps Total Possible Points - 132 Time Limit: 30 minutes	Practice #1	Practice #2	Practice #3	Final
27. Place an *X* in the YES box to indicate that the physician will accept Medicare or TRICARE assignment of benefits. The check will be sent directly to the physician.				
28. Enter the total charge for the service.				
29. Enter the amount already paid by any primary insurance company or the patient, if it pertains to his deductible. Do not enter payments by the patient if it pertains to the coinsurance amount. For primary Medicare claims, leave blank.*				
30. Enter the balance due your office (subtract field 29 from field 28 to obtain this figure). For primary Medicare claims, leave blank.				
31. Have the physician or service supplier sign and date the form here.*				
32. Enter the name and address of the organization or individual who performed the services. If performed in the patient's home, leave this field blank. 32a. In field 32a, enter the NPI for the service facility. 32b. Use field 32b if the facility does not yet have an NPI. In this case, enter the appropriate two-digit qualifier immediately followed by the identification number being used. Do not place any spaces or punctuation between the qualifier and the identification number.				
33. List the billing physician's or supplier's name, address, zip code, and phone number. 33a. In field 33a, enter the NPI of the billing provider. 33b. If the billing provider does not yet have an NPI, enter the non-NPI qualifier in field 33b immediately followed by the identification number being used.				
Total Number of Points Achieved/Final Score				
Initials of Observer:				

Comments and Signatures

Reviewer's comments and signatures:

1. ______________________________

2. ______________________________

3. ______________________________

Instructor's comments:

____

Name ______________________ Class ______________ Date __________

CHAPTER 16

Medical Coding

REVIEW

Vocabulary Review

Matching

Match the key terms in the right column with the definitions in the left column by placing the letter of each correct answer in the space provided.

_____ **1.** Codes used for healthy patients receiving routine services

_____ **2.** CPT codes used to report the physician's exam of a patient to diagnose conditions and determine a course of treatment

_____ **3.** A code that is used to report the services the physician provided for a patient, such as surgery

_____ **4.** The sixth section of CPT codes

_____ **5.** CPT codes used to report procedures done in addition to another procedure

_____ **6.** The person with the ultimate responsibility for proper documentation and correct coding as well as compliance with regulations

_____ **7.** A coding reference for patient diagnoses

_____ **8.** A coding reference for medical services performed by physicians

_____ **9.** A patient who has not received services from the physician within the last 3 years

_____ **10.** A list of abbreviations, punctuation guides, symbols, typefaces, and instructional notes that provide guidelines for using a code set

_____ **11.** A system developed by the Centers for Medicare and Medicaid Services (CMS) for use in coding services for Medicare patients

_____ **12.** Acts that take advantage of others for personal gain

a. add-on code
b. physician
c. conventions
d. *Current Procedural Terminology* (CPT)
e. V codes
f. E/M code
g. fraud
h. Health Care Common Procedure Coding System (HCPCS)
i. *International Classification of Diseases, Ninth Revision, Clinical Modification* (ICD-9)
j. new patient
k. procedure code
l. Medicine — 90281–99602

True or False

Decide whether each statement is true or false. In the space at the left, write T *for* true *or* F *for* false. *On the lines provided, rewrite the false statements to make them true.*

_____ **13.** To avoid the risk of fraud, medical offices have a compliance plan to uncover compliance problems and correct them.

____

_____ **14.** A diagnosis is a description of the patient's course of treatment.

____

_______ **15.** The Alphabetic Index of the ICD-9 is used to verify a code selection after it has been looked up in the Tabular List.

____

_______ **16.** An established patient has seen the physician within the previous three years before this visit.

____

_______ **17.** In correct claims, each reported service is connected to a diagnosis that supports the procedure as necessary to investigate or treat the patient's condition.

____

_______ **18.** During the global period, follow-up care related to the surgical procedure is included in the procedure payment from the insurance carrier.

____

_______ **19.** In selecting a code from the ICD-9, you can safely ignore all cross-references.

____

_______ **20.** A CPT modifier has three digits and a letter.

____

_______ **21.** The Health Care Common Procedure Coding System was developed to code workers' compensation claims.

____

_______ **22.** HIPAA calls for penalties for giving remuneration to anyone eligible for benefits under federal health-care programs.

____

_______ **23.** Evaluation and management codes (E/M codes) are often considered the most important of all CPT codes because they can be used by all physicians in any medical specialty.

____

Content Review

Multiple Choice

In the space provided, write the letter of the choice that best completes each statement or answers each question.

_______ **1.** ICD-9 and CPT coding reference books are updated

A. annually.
B. quarterly.
C. monthly.
D. every five years.
E. as needed.

_______ **2.** The most specific diagnosis code has

A. three digits.
B. four digits.
C. five digits.
D. five digits and a modifier.

_______ **3.** Brackets—[ ]—are used around

A. descriptions that do not affect the code

B. instructions.

C. descriptions that do not affect the code.

D. an incomplete term.

E. synonyms, alternative wordings, or explanations.

_______ **4.** Where in CPT would you look for guidelines on using each section?

A. The preface

B. The notes at the beginning of each section

C. The appendixes

D. The descriptions next to each code

_______ **5.** The abbreviation NOS means

A. no other symbol.

B. not otherwise specified.

C. not often seen.

D. nearest order sequence.

_______ **6.** Injections and immunizations require two codes: one for giving the injection and the second for

A. the E/M.

B. the substance.

C. the V code.

D. the global period.

E. the evaluation.

_______ **7.** In the Health Care Common Procedure Coding System (HCPCS), which codes duplicate the CPT?

A. Level I

B. Level II

C. Category II

D. Category III

E. All of the above

_______ **8.** CPT codes are made up of

A. three digits.

B. four digits.

C. five digits.

D. six digits.

Sentence Completion

In the space provided, write the word or phrase that best completes each sentence.

9. When choosing the diagnosis code for the health-care claim, the most specific code should be used by utilizing _______ digits when available.

10. To find the correct ICD-9-CM code, begin by looking up the main term in the _______.

11. _______ codes are used to track health-care performance measures, such as programs and counseling to avoid tobacco use.

9. ______________________________

10. ______________________________

11. ______________________________

12. A(n) _______ code for accidental poisoning is selected from the ICD-9 manual.

13 The period of time that is covered for follow-up care is called the _______.

14. The connection between the diagnostic and the procedural information is called the code _______.

15. The next revision of the diagnostic code set is called the ICD- _______ -CM.

16. When unbundling is done intentionally to receive more payment than is correct, the claim is likely to be considered _______.

17. The codes in the ICD-9 Tabular List are organized according to the source or _______ system.

12. ________________

13. ________________

14. ________________

15. ________________

16. ________________

17. ________________

Short Answer

Write the answer to each question on the lines provided.

18. List the six sections of the CPT coding reference.

____

____

____

19. List the three indexes provided by the alphabetical index.

____

____

____

20. List the five steps involved with selecting a correct ICD-9-CM code.

____

____

____

21. List the three key factors that determine the level of an evaluation and management (E/M) service.

____

____

____

22. List the five steps involved with selecting a correct CPT code.

____

____

____

Name ______________________ Class ______________ Date ____________

Critical Thinking

Write the answer to each question on the lines provided.

1. Why is accurate coding important?

2. Why is billing for services that are not provided considered fraud? Why can't it be considered just a mistake or an error?

3. Why are medical offices advised to keep the previous year's code books?

4. What is the ultimate goal or desired outcome of medical coding?

APPLICATION

Follow the directions for each application.

1. **Becoming Familiar with ICD-9-CM**

   Work with a partner. Use the most recent ICD-9-CM reference available to you.

   a. Using Appendix E of the ICD-9-CM, select four of the three-digit disease categories to study, such as iron deficiency anemias, chronic pulmonary heart disease, and diabetes mellitus.

   b. Study the entries for the selected category in the Tabular List. Make a note of the appearance of any conventions. If a *code also underlying condition* instruction is found, research the possible choice.

   c. Prepare a report of the codes that require fourth or fifth digits in each of the categories.

2. **Becoming Familiar with CPT**

   Work with a partner. Use the most recent CPT reference available to you.

   a. In the Surgery Section of the CPT, find the heading "Subsection Information" in the Surgery Guidelines.

   b. Read the subsection notes for Removal of Skin Tags, Shaving of Lesions, Excision—Benign Lesions, and Excision—Malignant Lesions, analyzing the type of instructions provided.

   c. Prepare a comparison table of the instructions of the four subsection notes, covering these topics:

   - Definition of Method
   - Type of Anesthesia Covered

- Use of Lesion Size to Select Code
- Instructions on Modifiers

Case Studies

Write your response to each case study on the lines provided.

Case 1

A patient with acute appendicitis with generalized peritonitis had an appendectomy that was performed using laparoscopy. What procedure code and diagnosis code would you report?

____

____

____

Case 2

A 64-year-old male patient presented for his annual complete physical exam. A routine 12-lead electrocardiogram (ECG) and a general health panel laboratory test were also performed. What procedure codes and diagnosis code would you report on a health-care claim for this service?

____

____

____

Case 3

A patient presented for evaluation after a fainting spell. The following tests were ordered by the physician: carbon dioxide, chloride, potassium, and sodium. The health-care claim that was submitted contained procedure codes for each test. You have not received any payment on this claim, although payments for other claims sent to the same carrier on that day have been received. What do you think accounts for the delay?

____

____

____

Procedure Competency Checklists

Procedure 16.1 Locating an ICD-9-CM Code

Procedure Goal

To analyze diagnoses and locate the correct ICD code.

Scoring System

To score each step, use the following scoring system:
1 = poor, 2 = fair, 3 = good, 4 = excellent

A minimum score of at least a 3 must be achieved on **each** step to achieve successful completion of the technique. Detailed instructions on the scoring system are found on page x of the Preface.

Materials

Patient record, charge slip or superbill, ICD-9-CM manual

Name ______________________ Class ______________ Date ____________

Procedure

Procedure Steps Total Possible Points - 20 Time Limit: 10 minutes	Practice #1	Practice #2	Practice #3	Final
1. Locate the patient's diagnosis. a. This information may be located on the superbill (encounter form) or elsewhere in the patient's chart. If it is on the superbill, verify documentation in the medical chart.*				
2. Find the diagnosis in the ICD's Alphabetic Index. Look for the condition first, then locate the indented subterms that make the condition more specific. Read all cross-references to check all the possibilities for a term, including its synonyms and any eponyms.*				
3. Locate the code from the Alphabetic Index in the ICD's Tabular List.*				
4. Read all information to find the code that corresponds to the patient's specific disease or condition. a. Study the list of codes and descriptions. Be sure to pick the most specific code available. Check for the symbol that shows that a four- or five-digit code is required.*				
5. Carefully record the diagnosis code(s) on the insurance claim and proofread the numbers. a. Be sure that all necessary codes are given to completely describe each diagnosis. Check for instructions stating an additional code is needed. If more than one code is needed, be sure instructions are followed and the codes are listed in the correct order.*				
Total Number of Points Achieved/Final Score				
Initials of Observer:				

Comments and Signatures

Reviewer's comments and signatures:

1. ______________________________

2. ______________________________

3. ______________________________

Instructor's comments:

____

Procedure 16.2 Locating a CPT Code

Procedure Goal

To locate correct CPT codes

Scoring System

To score each step, use the following scoring system:
1 = poor, 2 = fair, 3 = good, 4 = excellent

Name ______________________ Class ______________ Date ________

A minimum score of at least a 3 must be achieved on **each** step to achieve successful completion of the technique. Detailed instructions on the scoring system are found on page x of the Preface.

Materials

Patient record, superbill or charge slip, CPT manual

Procedure

Procedure Steps Total Possible Points - 20 Time Limit: 10 minutes	Practice #1	Practice #2	Practice #3	Final
1. Find the services listed on the superbill (if used) and in the patient's record. a. Check the patient's record to see which services were documented. For E/M procedures, look for clues as to the location of the service, extent of history, exam, and medical decision making that were involved.* 2. Look up the procedure code(s) in the alphabetic index of the CPT manual. a. Verify the code number in the numeric index, reading all notes and guidelines for that section. b. If a code range is noted, look up the range and choose the correct code from the range given. If the correct description is not found, start the process again. Use the same process if multiple codes are given.* 3. Determine appropriate modifiers. a. Check section guidelines and Appendix A to choose a modifier if needed to explain a situation involving the procedure being coded, such as bilateral procedure, surgical team, or a discontinued procedure.* 4. Carefully record the procedure code(s) on the health-care claim. Usually the primary procedure, the one that is the primary reason for the encounter or visit, is listed first.* 5. Match each procedure with its corresponding diagnosis. The primary procedure is often (but not always) matched with the primary diagnosis.*				
Total Number of Points Achieved/Final Score				
Initials of Observer:				

Comments and Signatures

Reviewer's comments and signatures:

1. ______________________

2. ______________________

3. ______________________

Instructor's comments:

____

Name ______________________ Class ______________ Date __________

CHAPTER 17

Patient Billing and Collections

REVIEW

Vocabulary Review

Matching

Match the key terms in the right column with the definitions in the left column by placing the letter of each correct answer in the space provided.

_______ 1. An account with only one charge

_______ 2. An organization that manages delinquent accounts

_______ 3. A written description of the agreed terms of payment

_______ 4. An act that prohibits certain collection tactics, such as harassment

_______ 5. The process of classifying and reviewing past-due accounts by age from the first date of billing

_______ 6. An act that requires credit bureaus to supply correct and complete information to businesses for use in evaluating a person's application for credit, insurance, or a job

_______ 7. A law that sets a time limit on when a collection suit on a past-due account can legally be filed

_______ 8. An act that requires creditors to provide applicants with accurate and complete credit costs and terms

_______ 9. The court-decreed right to make decisions about a child's upbringing

_______ 10. According to this organization, it is appropriate to assess finance charges or late charges on past-due accounts if the patient is notified in advance

_______ 11. An account that is open to charges made occasionally

a. age analysis
b. Fair Credit Reporting Act
c. AMA
d. disclosure statement
e. legal custody
f. Truth in Lending Act
g. single-entry account
h. open-book account
i. statute of limitations
j. Fair Debt Collection Practices Act of 1977
k. collection agency

True or False

Decide whether each statement is true or false. In the space at the left, write T *for true or* F *for false. On the lines provided, rewrite the false statements to make them true.*

_______ 12. Immediate payment from patients brings income into the practice and saves the cost of preparing and mailing bills.

____

_______ 13. Most physicians prefer to collect payments from patients at the end of each month.

____

_______ **14.** The one major disadvantage to the use of credit cards in a medical practice is cost to the practice.

____

_______ **15.** A billing cycle is a common billing system that requires that all the billing be done in the last week of every month.

____

_______ **16.** The price list for a medical practice is called a charge slip.

____

Content Review

Multiple Choice

In the space provided, write the letter of the choice that best completes each statement or answers each question.

_______ **1.** A superbill

A. includes the charges for services rendered on that day.
B. is given to the doctor after he sees the patient.
C. is inappropriate if the patient has insurance.
D. is mailed to the patient when the account is 30 days past due.
E. is always completed electronically.

_______ **2.** A practice may buy accounts receivable insurance to protect the practice from

A. welfare patients.
B. employee theft.
C. lost income because of nonpayment.
D. malpractice.

_______ **3.** The Fair Debt Collection Practices Act of 1977

A. allows you to call patients at any time to get payment.
B. permits you to threaten to turn the account over to collections.
C. permits you to harass the patient daily for payment.
D. governs the methods that can be used to collect unpaid debts.

_______ **4.** Free treatment for hardship cases is

A. up to the receptionist to allow.
B. expected by all patients in all cases.
C. at the doctor's discretion.
D. never permitted.
E. based on the patient's credit report

_______ **5.** The best form of payment in a medical office is

A. insurance.
B. debit card.
C. check.
D. credit card.
E. All of the above.

Name ______________________ Class ______________ Date ____________

_______ 6. A hardship case is defined as a person who is
- A. poor.
- B. underinsured.
- C. uninsured.
- D. All of the above.

_______ 7. The purpose of an age analysis is to
- A. determine which accounts to turn over to collections.
- B. determine how much money is owed to the practice and how long it has been outstanding.
- C. classify and review past-due accounts.
- D. All of the above.

_______ 8. Most practices begin the collection process with
- A. telephone calls, home visits, or letters.
- B. contracts or age analyses.
- C. credit checks, letters, or statements.
- D. credit checks or collection agencies.
- E. telephone calls, letters, or statements.

_______ 9. Which of the following organizations offers certification for coding specialists?
- A. AMA
- B. AHIMA
- C. AAPC
- D. Both B and C
- E. Both A and C

Sentence Completion

In the space provided, write the word or phrase that best completes each sentence.

10. Money paid as punishment for intentionally breaking the law is referred to as _______. 10. ______________

11. The Truth in Lending Act covers credit agreements that involve more than _______ payments. 11. ______________

12. A _______ provides information about the credit worthiness of a person seeking credit. 12. ______________

13. This act prevents you from calling the patient before 8 AM or after 9 PM to request payment. 13. ______________

14. Health insurance for dependents of active-duty and retired military personnel is provided by _______. 14. ______________

15. When a physician treats other doctors for free, it is referred to as extending a _______. 15. ______________

16. A _______ is the average fee charged by all comparable doctors in the region. 16. ______________

17. A _______ is a price list for the medical practice. 17. ______________

Name ______________________ Class ______________ Date __________

Short Answer

Write the answer to each question on the lines provided.

18. Describe what cycle billing means.

19. What is the purpose of using RVUs?

20. When determining the responsibilities for minors, the parent who has legal custody can make what type of decisions?

21. In an open-book account, does the time limit for collection begin when the account is initiated? Why or why not?

22. How would you compute gross collection percentage?

Critical Thinking

Write the answer to each question on the lines provided.

1. A patient is through seeing the doctor and he hands you his charge slip for services. You ask how he would like to pay. He hands you a credit card that the practice does not accept. What do you say?

2. The physician has asked you to make some phone calls to request payment on delinquent accounts. What collection practices should you follow to avoid harassing behaviors or breaking the law?

Name ______________________ Class ______________ Date ______________

3. When handing a patient's account over to a collection agency, what information should you supply about the patient?

4. Your medical practice is using a collection agency to collect past-due accounts. You receive a phone call from a patient who states that he has been contacted by the collection agency agent, who made threats to the patient. What do you do?

5. Imagine that the doctor in your office is extending credit to a patient. What are the benefits of extending credit?

Application

Follow the directions for the application.

Using the knowledge gained in the text, including Chapter 17, design a charge table or form that clearly defines each type of office care. Include such information as (a) is the patient a new patient, (b) is the patient an established patient, (c) was the appointment simply a consultation, (d) did the patient receive limited care, (e) did the patient receive comprehensive care, and so on. Define each type of care in detail so as to avoid any billing questions. A patient may come to you and argue that the type of care she received was "limited" and the physician checked "comprehensive" on the bill. You will need this form to show the patient exactly which services are given under each type of care.

Case Studies

Write your response to each case study on the lines provided.

Case 1

A patient comes to you to pay for his office visit. He hands you the check and says he is in a hurry and cannot wait for a receipt. He leaves and you notice he has not signed the check. What do you do?

Case 2

You are making collection calls. You call a patient and reach the patient's wife. You are told the patient is not there. The wife seems anxious to assist you and asks if she can help. What do you do?

Name ______________________ Class ______________ Date ______________

Procedure Competency Checklist

PROCEDURE 17.1 HOW TO BILL WITH THE SUPERBILL

Procedure Goal

To complete a superbill accurately

Scoring System

To score each step, use the following scoring system:
1 = poor, 2 = fair, 3 = good, 4 = excellent

A minimum score of at least a 3 must be achieved on **each** step to achieve successful completion of the technique. Detailed instructions on the scoring system are found on page x of the Preface.

Materials

Superbill, patient ledger card, patient information sheet, fee schedule, insurance code list, pen

Procedure

Procedure Steps Total Possible Points - 48 Time Limit: 10 minutes	Practice #1	Practice #2	Practice #3	Final
1. Make sure the doctor's name and address appear on the form.*				
2. From the patient ledger card and information sheet, fill in the patient data, such as name, sex, date of birth, and insurance information.				
3. Fill in the place and date of service.				
4. Attach the superbill to the patient's medical record and give them both to the doctor.*				
5. Accept the completed superbill from the patient after the patient sees the doctor. Make sure that the doctor has indicated the diagnosis and the procedures performed. Also make sure that an appropriate diagnosis is listed for each procedure.*				
6. If the doctor has not already recorded the charges, refer to the fee schedule for procedures that are marked. Then fill in the charges next to those procedures.*				
7. In the appropriate blanks, list the total charges for the visit and the previous balance (if any).				
8. Calculate the subtotal.				
9. Fill in the amount and type of payment (cash, check, money order, or credit card) made by the patient during this visit.*				
10. Calculate and enter the new balance.				
11. Have the patient sign the authorization-and-release section of the superbill.*				

(continued)

Name ______________________ Class ______________ Date ____________

Procedure Steps Total Possible Points - 48 Time Limit: 10 minutes	Practice #1	Practice #2	Practice #3	Final
12. Keep a copy of the superbill for the practice records. Give the original to the patient along with one copy to file with the insurer.*				
Total Number of Points Achieved/Final Score				
Initials of Observer:				

Comments and Signatures

Reviewer's comments and signatures:

1. ______________________________

2. ______________________________

3. ______________________________

Instructor's comments:

____

Name ______________________ Class ______________ Date ________

CHAPTER 18

Accounting for the Medical Office

Review

Vocabulary Review

Matching

Match the key terms in the right column with the definitions in the left column by placing the letter of each correct answer in the space provided.

_______ 1. A chronological list of the charges to patients and the payments received from patients each day

_______ 2. The total amount of income earned before deductions

_______ 3. Money set aside to pay taxes to appropriate government agencies

_______ 4. A system that allows you to handle the practice's payroll without writing payroll checks manually

_______ 5. Federal Tax Deposit (FTD) coupon

_______ 6. Systematic recording of business transactions

_______ 7. The party who writes the check

_______ 8. Legally transferable from one person to another

_______ 9. Appears as a fraction on the upper edge of all printed checks

_______ 10. Shows the total owed to the practice

_______ 11. The original record of the doctor's services and the charge for those services

_______ 12. Lets you write each transaction once while recording it on four different bookkeeping forms

_______ 13. Business checks with stubs attached

_______ 14. A blank check that allows the depositor to withdraw funds from her account only

_______ 15. A legal agreement between two or more people to perform an act in exchange for payment

_______ 16. Employer's annual federal unemployment (FUTA) tax return

a. tax liability
b. ABA number
c. employment contract
d. charge slip
e. EFTS
f. Form 940
g. gross earning
h. Form 941
i. accounts receivable record
j. daily log
k. payer
l. bookkeeping
m. Form 8109
n. pegboard system
o. counter check
p. negotiable
q. voucher checks

Name ______________________ Class ______________ Date ____________

True or False

Decide whether each statement is true or false. In the space at the left, write T *for true or* F *for false. On the lines provided, rewrite the false statements to make them true.*

_______ **17.** Medical assistants should obtain information for the daily log from word of mouth from patients.

____

_______ **18.** Reconciliation means to compare the records of the medical practice with the records of the patient.

____

_______ **19.** To help with the practice's bookkeeping and banking, you need to understand basic accounting systems and have certain financial management skills.

____

_______ **20.** After accepting a check, you should set it carefully aside for the endorsement process, which should be done in a batch with other checks.

____

_______ **21.** All bookkeeping systems include records of income, charges (money owed to the practice), and disbursements (money paid out by the practice).

____

_______ **22.** To calculate net earning, you should subtract total deductions from gross earnings.

____

_______ **23.** A check would be nonnegotiable if it is signed.

____

_______ **24.** SUTA taxes are payable to the federal government.

____

_______ **25.** Information on a patient ledger card includes the patient's name, address, phone number(s), and the name of the person responsible for the charges (if different from the patient).

____

_______ **26.** Managing payroll does not fall within the medical assistant's scope of practice.

____

_______ **27.** FICA taxes fund Social Security and Medicare.

____

Content Review

Multiple Choice

In the space provided, write the letter of the choice that best completes each statement or answers each question.

_______ **1.** The purpose of the daily log is to

A. provide a record of each patient seen.
B. list appointments.
C. reconcile all finances.
D. None of the above.

_______ **2.** If the medical practice uses a payroll service,
- **A.** you don't have any responsibilities for payroll.
- **B.** you may supply time cards or payroll data to the service.
- **C.** you will still have to calculate the deductions.
- **D.** you will still have to write the checks.
- **E.** you will still have to mail the checks.

_______ **3.** The patient ledger card does not include the patient's
- **A.** name.
- **B.** insurance policy number.
- **C.** driver's license number.
- **D.** work number.

_______ **4.** For FICA tax, you should withhold from the employee's check
- **A.** half of the tax owed for the pay period.
- **B.** one-third of the tax owed for the pay period.
- **C.** one-quarter of the tax owed for the pay period.
- **D.** all of the tax owed for the pay period.

_______ **5.** The double-entry accounting system is based on the following accounting equation:
- **A.** Assets = Liabilities + Owner Equity
- **B.** Liabilities = Assets + Owner Equity
- **C.** Owner Equity = Assets + Liabilities
- **D.** None of the above

_______ **6.** Most bookkeeping software programs include
- **A.** grammar and spell-check features.
- **B.** built-in tax tables.
- **C.** electronic endorsements.
- **D.** built-in check codes.

_______ **7.** Federal unemployment tax is
- **A.** not paid by the practice.
- **B.** paid by the employee.
- **C.** not a deduction from employees' paychecks.
- **D.** not based on the employees, earnings.

_______ **8.** In which of the following denominations are travelers' checks printed?
- **A.** $5, $10, $20, $50, $100
- **B.** $5, $10, $20, $50
- **C.** $5, $10, $20, $50, $100, $500
- **D.** $10, $20, $50, $100
- **E.** $10, $20, $50, $100, $500

_______ **9.** The employee's payroll information sheet
- **A.** is maintained by the employee.
- **B.** does not include the employee's hourly wage rate.
- **C.** must maintain up-to-date, accurate payroll information about each employee.
- **D.** None of the above.

Name ______________________________ Class ____________________ Date ______________

Sentence Completion

In the space provided, write the word or phrase that best completes each sentence.

10. An accounts payable record shows the amounts the practice owes to _______.

11. The _______ shows how much cash is available to cover expenses, invest, or take as profits.

12. Whereas assets are goods or properties that are part of the worth of a practice, liabilities are amounts owed by the practice to _______.

13. An EIN is _______.

14. A person who receives a check is known as a _______.

15. The ABA number on a printed check is a bank identification number that appears in the form of a fraction on the _______ of the check.

16. A medical assistant receives an additional $40 in her paycheck for a week in which she worked an extra hour every day. This makes her payroll type _______.

17. To replenish petty cash, you should write a check payable to _______.

10. ______________________________

11. ______________________________

12. ______________________________

13. ______________________________

14. ______________________________

15. ______________________________

16. ______________________________

17. ______________________________

Short Answer

Write the answer to each question on the lines provided.

18. Describe the importance of accuracy in bookkeeping and banking.

19. What is the purpose of Form 941?

20. What are some of the expenses recorded in the accounts payable records?

21. Why is it advantageous to make frequent bank deposits?

22. What should you do if you cannot read the handwriting on a check?

23. What are four things you can find out by telephone banking?

24. How do you start a petty cash fund?

Critical Thinking

Write the answer to each question on the lines provided.

1. What is the purpose of a deposit slip?

2. Why is it important to reconcile the monthly bank statement with your checkbook balance?

3. Name some of the information listed on the patient ledger card and why each is important to keep up-to-date.

4. Who is inconvenienced or harmed when there is a bookkeeping error?

Name ______________________ Class ______________ Date __________

Application

Follow the directions for the application.

Using a ledger sheet—either one purchased in an office supply store or one made up on the computer—create a record of office disbursements for a one-month period using the following information.

a. For the purposes of this exercise, use November 2008. Remember that you'll need a column for the date, payee, check number, and total amount plus each of the expenses listed here. You decide which check number to begin with.

b. Types of Expenses

- rent
- utilities
- postage
- lab/x-rays
- medical supplies
- office supplies
- wages
- insurance
- taxes
- travel
- miscellaneous

c. Monthly Expenses

Use this information to fill in your office disbursements ledger.

- 11/01 – Payment to La Jolla Property Management for rent, $1700.00.
- 11/01 – Payment to Anderson Janitorial for monthly office cleaning, $850.00.
- 11/01 – Office Depot for fax machine paper, $37.89.
- 11/01 – Pacific Telephone for monthly telephone services, $384.57.
- 11/01 – Pacific Gas Company for monthly gas and electric, $683.84.
- 11/01 – Cash for stamps at the post office, $32.00.
- 11/02 – Uni Lab for blood work, $55.00.
- 11/02 – Harris Medical Supply for general medical supplies, $75.00.
- 11/05 – Medi Quik X-Ray, $32.50.
- 11/06 – Staples Office Supply for general office supplies, $68.24.
- 11/12 – City Laundry (uniforms and towels), $125.00.
- 11/15 – Toni Guzzi (payroll), $76.08.
- 11/15 – Terry Smart (payroll), $89.84.
- 11/15 – Janet Garcia (payroll), $125.00.
- 11/15 – James Smith (payroll), $78.76.
- 11/17 – Toni Guzzi (reimbursement for travel expenses), $12.50.
- 11/20 – Stamps at post office from petty cash, $64.00.
- 11/23 – Medi Quik X-Ray, $35.87.
- 11/25 – World Wide Insurance, $189.00
- 11/30 – IRS, $537.00.

d. Be sure your amounts at the total of your record agree with the amounts in each of the accounts.

Name ______________________ Class ______________ Date ____________

Case Studies

Write your response to each case study on the lines provided.

Case 1

You are a senior medical assistant in a physician's office in charge of all the bookkeeping and banking tasks. You decided to take a couple of days off and handed your duties off to a less experienced medical assistant. All she needed to do was make the Friday deposit at the bank, and you were supposed to call her on Friday to be sure it was done. You wake up in the middle of the night and are startled to remember that you forgot to call and help her through the process. What methods would you use to determine if the deposit had been made correctly?

____

____

____

Case 2

Your bank statement has arrived in the mail and along with it is a check from a patient marked "Insufficient Funds." What does this mean, and what do you do now to get paid?

____

____

____

Case 3

Your bank statement has arrived in the mail and the balance from the bank does not agree with the balance in your check register. What do you do?

____

____

____

Procedure Competency Checklists

Procedure 18.1 Organizing the Practice's Bookkeeping System

Procedure Goal

To maintain a bookkeeping system that promotes accurate record keeping for the practice

Scoring System

To score each step, use the following scoring system:
1 = poor, 2 = fair, 3 = good, 4 = excellent

A minimum score of at least a 3 must be achieved on **each** step to achieve successful completion of the technique. Detailed instructions on the scoring system are found on page x of the Preface.

Materials

Daily log sheets, patient ledger cards, and check register, or computerized bookkeeping system; summaries of charges, receipts, and disbursements

Name ______________________ Class ______________ Date __________

Procedure

Procedure Steps Total Possible Points - 20 Time Limit: 10 minutes	Practice #1	Practice #2	Practice #3	Final
1. Use a new daily log sheet each day. For each patient seen that day, record the patient name, the relevant charges, and any payments received, calculating any necessary adjustments and new balances. If you're using a computerized system, enter the patient's name, the relevant charges, and any payments received and adjustments made in the appropriate areas. The computer will calculate the new balances.*				
2. Create a ledger card for each new patient and maintain a ledger card for all existing patients. The ledger card should include the patient's name, address, home and work telephone numbers, and insurance company. It should also contain the name of the person responsible for the charges (if different from the patient). Update the ledger card every time the patient incurs a charge or makes a payment. Be sure to adjust the account balance after every transaction. In a computerized system, a patient record is the same as a ledger card. This record must also be maintained and updated.*				
3. Record all deposits accurately in the check register. File the deposit receipt—with a detailed listing of checks and money orders deposited—for later use in reconciling the bank statement. The deposit amount should match the amount of money collected by the practice for that day.				
4. When paying bills for the practice, enter each check in the check register accurately, including the check number, date, payee, and amount before writing the check.*				
5. Prepare and/or print a summary of charges, receipts, and disbursements every month, quarter, or year, as directed. Be sure to double-check all entries and calculations from the monthly summary before posting them to the quarterly summary. Also, double-check the entries and calculations from the quarterly summary before posting them to the yearly summary.*				
Total Number of Points Achieved/Final Score				
Initials of Observer:				

Comments and Signatures

Reviewer's comments and signatures:

1. ______________________________

2. ______________________________

3. ______________________________

Instructor's comments:

____

Name ______________________ Class ______________ Date __________

Procedure 18.2 Making a Bank Deposit

Procedure Goal

To prepare cash and checks for deposit and to deposit them properly into a bank account

Scoring System

To score each step, use the following scoring system:
1 = poor, 2 = fair, 3 = good, 4 = excellent

A minimum score of at least a 3 must be achieved on **each** step to achieve successful completion of the technique. Detailed instructions on the scoring system are found on page x of the Preface.

Materials

Bank deposit slip and items to be deposited, such as checks, cash, and money orders

Procedure

Procedure Steps Total Possible Points - 40 Time Limit: 10 minutes	Practice #1	Practice #2	Practice #3	Final
1. Divide the bills, coins, checks, and money orders into separate piles.				
2. Sort the bills by denomination, from largest to smallest. Then, stack them, portrait side up, in the same direction. Total the amount of the bills and write this amount on the deposit slip on the line marked "Currency."*				
3. If you have enough coins to fill coin wrappers, put them in wrappers of the proper denomination. If not, count the coins and put them in the deposit bag. Total the amount of coins and write this amount on the deposit slip on the line marked "Coin."				
4. Review all checks and money orders to be sure they are properly endorsed with a restrictive endorsement. List each check on the deposit slip, including the check number and amount. If you do not keep a list of the check writers' names in the office, record this information on the deposit slip also.				
5. List each money order on the deposit slip. Include the notation "money order" or "MO" and the name of the writer.				
6. Calculate the total deposit (total of amounts for currency, coin, checks, and money orders). Write this amount on the deposit slip on the line marked "Total." Photocopy the deposit slip for your office records.*				
7. Record the total amount of the deposit in the office checkbook register.*				
8. If you plan to make the deposit in person, place the currency, coins, checks, and money orders in a deposit bag. If you cannot make the deposit in person, put the checks and money orders in a special bank-by-mail envelope or put all deposit items in an envelope and send it by registered mail.				
9. Make the deposit in person or by mail.				

(continued)

Name ______________________ Class ______________ Date __________

Procedure Steps Total Possible Points - 40 Time Limit: 10 minutes	Practice #1	Practice #2	Practice #3	Final
10. Obtain a deposit receipt from the bank. File it with the copy of the deposit slip in the office for later use when reconciling the bank statement.*				
Total Number of Points Achieved/Final Score				
Initials of Observer:				

Comments and Signatures

Reviewer's comments and signatures:

1. ______________________

2. ______________________

3. ______________________

Instructor's comments:

____

Procedure 18.3 Reconciling a Bank Statement

Procedure Goal

To ensure that the bank record of deposits, payments, and withdrawals agrees with the practice's record of deposits, payments, and withdrawals

Scoring System

To score each step, use the following scoring system:
1 = poor, 2 = fair, 3 = good, 4 = excellent

A minimum score of at least a 3 must be achieved on **each** step to achieve successful completion of the technique. Detailed instructions on the scoring system are found on page x of the Preface.

Materials

Previous bank statement, current bank statement, reconciliation worksheet (if not part of current bank statement), deposit receipts, red pencil, check stubs or checkbook register, returned checks

Procedure

Procedure Steps Total Possible Points - 40 Time Limit: 15 minutes	Practice #1	Practice #2	Practice #3	Final
1. Check the closing balance on the previous statement against the opening balance on the new statement. The balances should match. If they do not, call the bank.				

(continued)

Name ______________________ Class ______________ Date __________

Procedure Steps Total Possible Points - 40 Time Limit: 15 minutes	Practice #1	Practice #2	Practice #3	Final
2. Record the closing balance from the new statement on the reconciliation worksheet (Figure 18-9). This worksheet usually appears on the back of the bank statement.				
3. Check each deposit receipt against the bank statement. Place a red check mark in the upper-right corner of each receipt that is recorded on the statement. Total the amount of deposits that do *not* appear on the statement. Add this amount to the closing balance on the reconciliation worksheet.*				
4. Put the returned checks in numerical order. (Your bank may send you several sheets consisting of photocopies of checks instead of the actual checks.)				
5. Compare each returned check with the bank statement, making sure that the amount on the check agrees with the amount on the statement. Place a red check mark in the upper-right corner of each returned check that is recorded on the statement. Also, place a check mark on the check stub or check register entry. Any checks that were written but that do not appear on the statement and were not returned are considered "outstanding" checks. You can find these easily on the check stubs or checkbook register because they have no red check mark.				
6. List each outstanding check separately on the worksheet, including its check number and amount. Total the outstanding checks and subtract this total from the bank statement balance.*				
7. If the statement shows that the checking account earned interest, add this amount to the checkbook balance.*				
8. If the statement lists such items as a service charge, check printing charge, or automatic payment, subtract them from the checkbook balance.*				
9. Compare the new checkbook balance with the new bank statement balance. They should match. If they do not, repeat the process, rechecking all calculations. Double-check the addition and subtraction in the checkbook register. Review the checkbook register to make sure you did not omit any items. Ensure that you carried the correct balance forward from one register page to the next. Double-check that you made the correct additions or subtractions for all interest earned and charges.				
10. If your work is correct, and the balances still do not agree, call the bank to determine if a bank error has been made. Contact the bank promptly because the bank may have a time limit for corrections. The bank may consider the bank statement correct if you do not point out an error within 2 weeks (or other period, according to bank policy).				

(continued)

Name ______________________ Class ______________ Date ____________

Procedure Steps Total Possible Points - 40 Time Limit: 15 minutes	Practice #1	Practice #2	Practice #3	Final

HOW TO BALANCE YOUR CHECKING ACCOUNT

1. Subtract any service charges that appear on this statement from your checkbook balance.
2. Add any interest paid on your checking account to your checkbook balance.
3. Check off (✔) in your checkbook register all checks and pre-authorized transactions listed on your statement.
4. Use the worksheet to list checks you have written, ATM withdrawals, and Point of Sale transactions which are not listed on your statement.

5. Enter the closing balance on the statement.	$	.
6. Add any deposits not shown on the statement.	+	.
7. Subtotal	$	.
8. Subtract total transactions outstanding (from worksheet on right).	–	.
9. Account balance (should match balance in your checkbook register).	$	.

IF YOUR ACCOUNT DOES NOT BALANCE

a. Check your addition and subtraction first on this form and then in your checkbook.
b. Be sure the deposit amounts on your statement are the same as those in your checkbook.
c. Be sure all the check amounts on your statement agree with the amounts entered in your checkbook register.
d. Be sure all checks written prior to this reconcilement period but not listed on the statement are listed on the worksheet.
e. Verify that all MAC® ATM, Point of Sale, and other pre-authorized transactions have been recorded in your checkbook register.
f. Review last month's statement to be certain any corrections were entered into your checkbook.

WORKSHEET
Transactions Outstanding

Number or Date	Amount
TOTAL	

Total Number of Points Achieved/Final Score				
Initials of Observer:				

Comments and Signatures

Reviewer's comments and signatures:

1. ______________________________

2. ______________________________

3. ______________________________

Instructor's comments:

____

Name ______________________________ Class ____________________ Date ____________

Procedure 18.4 Setting Up the Accounts Payable System

Procedure Goal

To set up an accounts payable system

Scoring System

To score each step, use the following scoring system:
1 = poor, 2 = fair, 3 = good, 4 = excellent

A minimum score of at least a 3 must be achieved on **each** step to achieve successful completion of the technique. Detailed instructions on the scoring system are found on page x of the Preface.

Materials

Disbursements journal, petty cash record, payroll register, pen

Procedure

Procedure Steps Total Possible Points - 48 Time Limit: 10 minutes	Practice #1	Practice #2	Practice #3	Final
Setting Up the Disbursements Journal				
1. Write in column headings for the basic information about each check: date, payee's name, check number, and check amount.				
2. Write in column headings for each type of business expense, such as rent and utilities.				
3. Write in column headings (if space is available) for deposits and the account balance.				
4. Record the data from completed checks under the appropriate column headings.				
Setting Up the Petty Cash Record				
1. Write in column headings for the date, transaction number, payee, brief description, amount of transaction, and type of expense.				
2. Write in a column heading (if space is available) for the petty cash fund balance.				
3. Record the data from petty cash vouchers under the appropriate column headings.				
Setting Up the Payroll Register				
1. Write in column headings for check number, employee name, earnings to date, hourly rate, hours worked, regular earnings, overtime hours worked, and overtime earnings.				
2. Write in column headings for total gross earnings for the pay period and gross taxable earnings.				
3. Write in column headings for each deduction. These may include federal income tax, Federal Insurance Contributions Act (FICA) tax, state income tax, local income tax, and various voluntary deductions.				

(continued)

Name ______________________ Class ______________ Date __________

Procedure Steps Total Possible Points - 48 Time Limit: 10 minutes	Practice #1	Practice #2	Practice #3	Final
4. Write in a column heading for net earnings.				
5. Each time you write payroll checks, record earning and deduction data under the appropriate column headings on the payroll register.				
Total Number of Points Achieved/Final Score				
Initials of Observer:				

Comments and Signatures

Reviewer's comments and signatures:

1. ______________________________

2. ______________________________

3. ______________________________

Instructor's comments:

____

Procedure 18.5 Generating Payroll

Procedure Goal

To handle the practice's payroll as efficiently and accurately as possible for each pay period

Scoring System

To score each step, use the following scoring system:
1 = poor, 2 = fair, 3 = good, 4 = excellent

A minimum score of at least a 3 must be achieved on **each** step to achieve successful completion of the technique. Detailed instructions on the scoring system are found on page x of the Preface.

Materials

Employees' time cards, employees' earnings records, payroll register, IRS tax tables, check register

Procedure

Procedure Steps Total Possible Points - 44 Time Limit: 15 minutes	Practice #1	Practice #2	Practice #3	Final
1. Calculate the total regular and overtime hours worked, based on the employee's time card. Enter those totals under the appropriate headings on the payroll register.*				
2. Check the pay rate on the employee earnings record. Then multiply the hours worked (including any paid vacation or paid holidays, if applicable) by the rates for regular time and overtime (time and a half or double time). This yields gross earnings.*				

(continued)

Name ______________________ Class ______________ Date __________

Procedure Steps Total Possible Points - 44 Time Limit: 15 minutes	Practice #1	Practice #2	Practice #3	Final
3. Enter the gross earnings under the appropriate heading on the payroll register. Subtract any nontaxable benefits, such as health-care or retirement programs.				
4. Using IRS tax tables and data on the employee earnings record, determine the amount of federal income tax to withhold based on the employee's marital status and number of exemptions. Also compute the amount of FICA tax to withhold for Social Security (6.2%) and Medicare (1.45%).*				
5. Following state and local procedures, determine the amount of state and local income taxes (if any) to withhold based on the employee's marital status and number of exemptions.*				
6. Calculate the employer's contributions to FUTA and to the state unemployment fund, if any. Post these amounts to the employer's account.				
7. Enter any other required or voluntary deductions, such as health insurance or contributions to a 401(k) fund.				
8. Subtract all deductions from the gross earnings to get the employee's net earnings.				
9. Enter the total amount withheld from all employees for FICA under the headings for Social Security and Medicare. Remember that the employer must match these amounts. Enter other employer contributions, such as for federal and state unemployment taxes, under the appropriate headings.*				
10. Fill out the check stub, including the employee's name, date, pay period, gross earnings, all deductions, and net earnings. Make out the paycheck for the net earnings.				
11. Deposit each deduction in a tax liability account.				
Total Number of Points Achieved/Final Score				
Initials of Observer:				

Comments and Signatures

Reviewer's comments and signatures:

1. ______________________________

2. ______________________________

3. ______________________________

Instructor's comments:

____

NOTES

NOTES

NOTES

NOTES